THE PSYCHIC SE
PERSONAL TRAIN

THE PSYCHIC SELF-DEFENSE PERSONAL TRAINING MANUAL

MARCIA L. PICKANDS

SAMUEL WEISER, INC.

York Beach, Maine

First published in 1997 by
Samuel Weiser, Inc.
Box 612
York Beach, ME 03910-0612

Library of Congress Cataloging-in-Publication Data

Pickands, Marcia.
    The psychic self-defense personal training manual / Marcia
Pickands.
        p. cm.
    Includes bibliographical references and index.
    ISBN 1-57863-004-5 (pbk..)
    1. Occultism. 2. Parapsychology. 3. Self-defense—Miscellanea.
I. Title.
BF1439.P56   1997
133.8—dc 21   96-40272
                                                                  CIP

BP

Typeset in 11 point Palatino

Cover illustration and text drawings by Tanith Pickands.
Cover design by Ray Rue.

Printed in the United States of America

03 02 01 00 99 98 97
10 9 8 7 6 5 4 3 2 1

I dedicate this book to the two men who taught me what I needed to know on this subject during this lifetime. They are Dr. Daniel K. Pai, the late Grandmaster of Pai Lum Kung Fu, and Wm. G. Gray, the founder of the Sangreal Sodality.

ACKNOWLEDGMENTS

I wish to thank my father, Dr. David C. Kellsey, for the start he gave me upon the Path to the Mysteries, my husband, Martin Pickands, for his never-failing support and mostly unflappable personal presence during this project, and the rest of my family and friends for putting up with me while this book was being written.

TABLE OF CONTENTS

LIST OF FIGURES AND TABLES

PREFACE

OVER THE YEARS, I have read every book that came my way on the topic of psychic self-defense and any others that included even a small section on this topic. Most of them were interesting, but inadequate for actual personal training. Most authors who have written books or articles on this subject appear to run into what I call the "DF dilemma" (the Dion Fortune dilemma). Dion Fortune's own words from her book, *Psychic Self-Defense*, illustrate my point: "It is hardly possible to give practical information on the methods of psychic defense without at the same time giving practical information on the methods of psychic attack. . . . To disclose sufficient to be adequate without disclosing sufficient to be dangerous is my [DF's] problem."[1] Murry Hope runs into this problem in her book, *Practical Techniques of Psychic Self-Defense*, but gets around it by indicating that only those who have been properly initiated have the ability to understand and use more "advanced" methods of psychic self-defense.[2] This lets her off the hook for any but the most basic information, which, to be fair, is as much as many people will ever need. However, no one knows if he or she will need more until a situation arises that demands it. Therefore, it is more sane to be overprepared than underprepared. Denning and Phillips, in their book, *Psychic Self-Defense & Well-*

[1] Dion Fortune, *Psychic Self-Defence* (London: Rider, 1930, and York Beach, ME: Samuel Weiser, 1992).
[2] Murry Hope, *Practical Techniques of Psychic Self-Defense* (New York: St. Martin's Press, 1985).

Being,[3] do an excellent job of explaining the basics, but their focus on the well-being end of things, and metaphysical/mystical theory and philosophy, tends to keep their book from being a straightforward psychic self-defense training manual.

My experience as a martial arts teacher has given me a different perspective. I have no objection to making information or training available to the general public, for it will better prepare people to defend and take care of themselves, as long as they practice. During the more than twenty years in which I have taught both physical and psychic self-defense, I have found that people who shouldn't know something because they are too "weak" in some way simply don't practice enough to do them any good, or any harm, and people who shouldn't know something because they may misuse it are going to find a way to do just that, whether I teach them or not. In fact, when I train people of the latter variety, I also convince them in no uncertain terms that there will always be someone "bigger and badder" out there than they are. In this way, they learn that it just might be better if they simply didn't get involved in the first place. The fear of information getting into the wrong hands simply keeps it out of the right hands!

As a purchaser of this book, you have the option of reading it or not reading it; practicing the exercises suggested or not; lending it to others; or contacting me through the publisher if you feel the call or need to know more. However, should you decide to read and work with the material presented in this manual, there are several things of which you should be aware:

1. I am not going to go into a great deal of detail about the various models of (or theories concerning) metaphysical reality. I am a firm believer in teaching through example and

---

[3] Melita Denning and Osborne Phillips, *Llewellyn Guide to Psychic Self-Defense & Well-Being* (St. Paul, MN: Llewellyn, 1983).

experience. Therefore, you will be given quite a number of exercises right up front. Try them! The experience you gain by doing this will be worth its weight in gold.

2. In writing this book, I am assuming that you already know something about psychic experience, metaphysics, magic, or the like. For this reason, I will not be spending a great deal of time explaining terms basic to these fields. However, for those of you not familiar with words or phrases such as: aura, third eye, centering, grounding, psychic/invisible body, physical/visible body, the magical elements (Air, Earth, Fire, and Water) and the like—don't panic or run for your nearest mystical dictionary! The exercises themselves explain most of these terms by example. Other terms are easily understood by reference to their context. In fact, I'll even give you a couple of brief definitions below just to make things easier:

A. *Aura:* The invisible part of you which interpenetrates your physical body and extends beyond it. It can be (and often is) broken down into any number of invisible bodies with different names and functions. However, all you need to do about this aura is act as if it exists until you practice the first exercise given at the beginning of chapter 1. That exercise will give you direct experience of how the aura/psychic body/invisible body, or bodies, can affect your physical body.

B. *Third Eye:* This is traditionally located on your forehead, between your eyebrows, and behind this position in your brain. It is only necessary to know this traditional position to correctly perform Exercise 1 (page 2), and all related exercises.

C. The magical elements are *Air, Fire, Water,* and *Earth.* Air is associated with the intellect and creativity. Fire is associated with passions, honor, and a knowledge of right and wrong. Water is associated with emotions. Earth is associated with basic physical needs and protection. There is a fifth element, known as Spirit. It is associated with the spiritual side of ourselves. Your aura has five psycho/spiritual organs (Spirit Center, Air Center, Fire Center, Water Center, and Earth Center) that are associated with the five magical elements. These will be experienced during the modified version of the Middle Pillar Exercise (page 20).

The best way to use this training manual is to imagine that you are actually participating in a course on psychic self-defense. As a student, your job is to follow the directions given to you in each and every exercise, and to treat the rest of the written material as if you were attending a lecture.

Especially during the first part of this book, exercises are given prior to explaining the whys and wherefores involved. It is important that you gain the experience first, so that you understand its importance at a deep level, before switching gears to pursue the more rational answers that your intellect will require. If you have questions, continue reading and most of them will be answered. It may take a little time and effort on your part to properly digest the material you have been given. Be patient with yourself. Keep a notebook to write down your experiences and any questions you may have. If, after several weeks of work, you still need answers, write me. I will answer all inquiries.[4]

Now that you know why I wrote this book and how to use it, please exercise your options to read and practice for the very best of reasons. May Divinity, by whatever name(s) you know It, guide you.

---

[4] Please write me in care of the publisher: c/o Samuel Weiser, Box 612, York Beach, ME 03910-0612, and all mail will be forwarded to me.

CHAPTER 1

WHY LEARN TO DEFEND YOURSELF PSYCHICALLY?

LIKE IT OR NOT, YOU must recognize that you are living in a world which is not always safe, physically or spiritually. In today's world, you would not hesitate to prepare yourself for work, play, or travel with an eye to your physical safety and you should be equally vigilant concerning your psychic/spiritual environment.

You are not just a soul embodied by matter; you are a soul with physical, mental, and spiritual bodies, all of which interpenetrate each other. What happens to one affects all others. For this reason, you must develop awareness on all levels of your being!

Here is an exercise which will show you in no uncertain terms how the invisible bodies that you carry around with you (nearly unconsciously) affect the visible/physical one which you take for granted. Ordinarily, this exercise is best demonstrated by someone familiar with the technique, however anyone can learn and make use of it. The first thing you need in order to practice this exercise is a partner who is about your size and strength. After you have snagged someone to help, simply follow these directions:

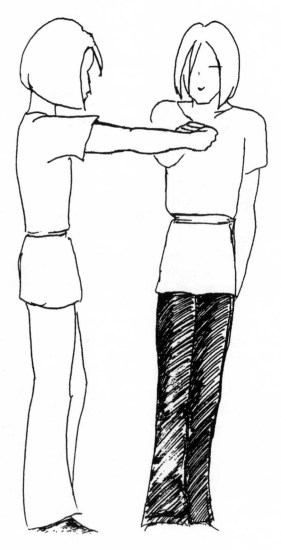

Figure 1. Assessing relative strength.

EXERCISE 1
Aura Stretching Exercise

1. Have your partner stand comfortably, facing you.

2. Have your partner raise the right arm to shoulder level, keeping it out straight, directly in front of the body, while forming the hand into a vertical fist, palm facing to the left, index finger at the top of the fist.

3. Position yourself so that your right shoulder is directly in front of the centerline of your partner's body, two to three feet away. Stand with your feet at shoulder's width and bend your knees slightly.

4. Place your right palm on your partner's outstretched right fist and ask him or her to resist upward as you press downward. This will establish the initial strength relationship between you. If your partner is considerably weaker than you are, you may press down with one or two fingers, instead of with your entire palm (see figure 1, page 2).

5. Take your right hand and cup it, with your palm facing away from your partner. Bring this hand down the centerline of your partner's body (about 4 inches from the body surface) from head to groin level. At this point, scoop your right hand away from your partner and past the left side of your body, before arching it up and then back over your head to the original position in front of your partner's head. Repeat this with increasing speed three to six more times, while visualizing yourself stretching your partner's normally invisible

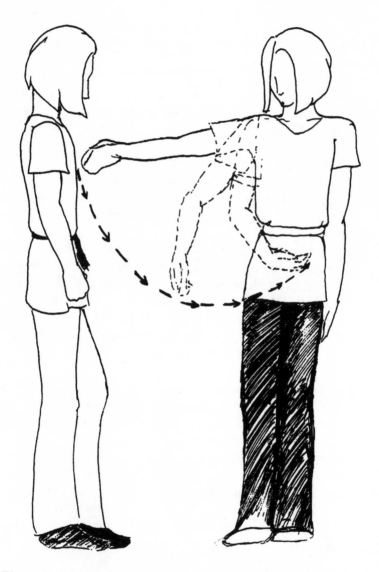

Figure 2. Manipulating your partner's psychic body.

psychic body/aura out and away. Finally, throw your right arm directly away from your partner's body while visualizing yourself hanging the outer edge of his or her psychic body up on the opposite wall or some other appropriate place several feet or more away from you both (see figure 2).

6. Repeat Step 4 and notice the difference. Your partner's arm should not be able to resist your pressure as well as it did originally and may indeed simply drop to the side. Why might this happen? (see figure 3, page 6).

7. Stand facing your partner and place your two thumbs together upon the center of his or her forehead (the third-eye area), while wrapping your fingers lightly around the head. Mentally unhook your partner's psychic body from wherever you left it and allow it to flow back through your body and thumbs into its original position (extending six to eight inches from your partner's physical body). Don't worry if it happens to settle slightly closer to your partner's body than it did originally (see figure 4, page 7).

8. Repeat Step 4 and notice the difference. Your strength, relative to your partner's, should be back to its original level, or your partner may feel slightly stronger than initially. Ask yourself why this happens.

9. Repeat Step 5 while asking your partner to assert mentally the following: "This is my energy and you may not take it away from me!"

10. Repeat Step 4 and notice the result. Your strength, relative to your partner's, should have remained at its original level.

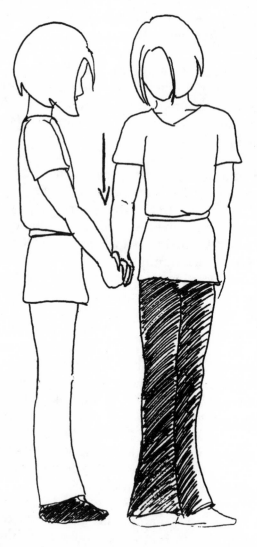

Figure 3. Reassessing your relative strength.

11. Reverse roles and allow your partner to try all of the above with you.

12. Try the same exercise using only the visualizations without the circular hand motions when you intend to stretch your partner's psychic body.

Figure 4. Returning your partner's psychic body.

This exercise should have demonstrated quite effectively that you are capable of affecting others physically without the necessity of physical contact. Only a person who is consciously blocking such an attempt, or who has well-developed mental and psychic shields, will be able to keep this from happening.

Learning the art of psychic self-defense is simply part of learning total self-defense. Even if all you wish to do is to prevent other people from unintentionally or deliberately draining your vital life force, you will need to gain knowledge of and proficiency in the art of psychic self-defense. I'm sure you know someone who can make you tired simply by being around and talking "at you" for more than five minutes. We all have this type of acquaintance or relative in our lives. Knowingly or not, this variety of individual is a psychic vampire! You can defend against them by choosing to learn to take care of yourself. This requires that you effectively discover, study, and explore body and mind through the media of soul and spirit, while simultaneously exploring the soul and spirit through the media of body and mind.

Most people would agree that we should be prepared to ward off or neutralize physical attacks against ourselves and our loved ones, but far too many people refuse to acknowledge the possibilities of attacks on any other level. They therefore never learn how to defend themselves fully. The power of "positive thinking" is all well and good, as is the theory that no one can harm you along spiritual lines unless you allow them to do so. The truth is that, unless you are trained to back up your "positive thinking" with effective technique, you are allowing others to control you by default. Since most of the evil that you will encounter in your lifetime will be generated by other humans, this can be a very dangerous oversight!

CHAPTER 2

THE BASICS
OF SELF-DEFENSE

THE EXERCISE THAT YOU learned in chapter 1 makes several things abundantly clear once you practice for a while:

1. A minor shift in your mental state can make a major difference in your apparent physical strength relative to other people.

2. Acting as if someone has what we think of as an invisible but very real psychic body or aura allows you to manipulate that psychic body at will. Doing so will also affect all other related bodies, unless the person you are attempting to work on actively prevents you from doing so through the use of his or her own mental commands or well-developed psychic shield.

3. If you are able to manipulate someone mentally and/or psychically with very little experience and practice, it stands to reason that you can also be manipulated that way by others.

Bearing these points in mind, practice Exercise 1 (page 2) for six months and then pick out a brand new partner. After your new partner has gained some success in preventing you from disturbing the psychic body by asserting mentally: "This is my energy and you may not take it away!" try it again, with the same assertion being made while you remind yourself silently that you have had more practice than your new partner has and can over-power him or her at will. You should have no trouble doing so!

You must be aware, when learning how to protect yourself psychically, that, although the techniques are not difficult, they require practice to make them powerful enough to be useful in most situations. After all, you can hardly be expected to walk around all day long mentally chanting, "This is my energy and no one can take it away from me." Technically you could do so, but you would get absolutely nothing else done. The idea is to make each tech-nique as easy and as natural as walking or talking. This means that you will have to practice each exercise until your subconscious mind takes over and handles the process involved automatically. We will start by modifying Exercise 1 (page 3) so that we can isolate the important fac-tors at work in it.

EXERCISE 2
Experiencing the Effects of Aura Displacement

1. Have your partner stand comfortably, facing you.

2. Have him or her raise the right arm to shoulder level, keeping it out straight, directly in front of the body, while forming the hand into a vertical fist, palm facing to the left, index finger at the top of the fist.

3. Position yourself so that your right shoulder is di-rectly in front of the centerline of your partner's body,

two to three feet away. Stand with your feet at shoulder's width and bend your knees slightly.

4. Place your right palm on your partner's outstretched right fist and ask him or her to resist upward as you press downward. This will establish the initial strength relationship between you. If your partner is considerably weaker than you are, you may press down with one or two fingers, instead of with your entire palm (see figure 1, page 2).

5. Take your right hand and cup it, with your palm facing away from your partner. Bring this hand down the centerline of your partner's body (about four inches from the body surface) from head to groin level. At this point, scoop your right hand away from your partner and past the left side of your body before arching it up and then back over your head to the original position in front of your partner's head. Repeat this with increasing speed three to six times, while visualizing yourself stretching your partner's normally invisible psychic body/aura out and away. Finally, throw your right arm directly away from your partner's body while visualizing yourself hanging the outer edge of his or her psychic body up on the opposite wall or some other appropriate place several feet or more away from you both (see figure 2, page 4).

6. Repeat Step 4 and notice the difference. Ask what your partner notices and/or feels (see figure 3, page 6).

7. Change places and repeat this exercise.

8. Practice this exercise until you both are very aware of what it feels like when someone is pulling on the energy belonging to your psychic body.

EXERCISE 3

Disciplining Your Aura to Remain in Place No Matter What Others Try to Do to You

1. Repeat Step 5 from Exercise 2 while asking your partner to assert mentally the following: "This is my energy and you may not take it away from me!"

2. Repeat Step 4 from Exercise 2 and notice the result. Your strength, relative to your partner's, should have returned to its original level. Ask what your partner felt and also relate what you felt.

3. Try this same exercise using only the visualizations, without the circular hand motions, when you intend to stretch your partner's psychic body. Tell each other what you feel.

4. Try the version of this exercise suggested in Step 3, but assert your power over your partner (mentally, of course). Who ended up the stronger? Practice until neither one of you can affect the other adversely.

5. Make sure you both practice each side of these exercises until you know the feeling of pulling in the energy of your psychic body so that it fully supports and protects your physical body, etc.

6. The next time you see your partner, ask him or her to assume the test position indicated in Exercise 2, Step 4; then see if you can disrupt the energy balance in your favor without any further warm-up. What happened? Practice this type of impromptu testing on each other until neither of you can affect the other adversely. This could take several months.

EXERCISE 4
Also known as Tanith's Exercise

1. Choose a partner who is unaware of your recent experiments. He or she should be quite obviously larger and stronger than you are, from a strictly physical point of view.

2. Ask this new partner to play a game of Indian arm wrestling with you, but add that you'd like to borrow some energy since he or she is so much bigger than you are.

3. If, and only if, your new partner agrees to this request voluntarily, mentally pull his or her psychic body past your body and hang it up on the wall behind you. Then arm wrestle. Note what happens. Should you merely tie, try again and mentally assert that you are adding enough of your partner's inner strength to yours in order to win the match.

4. Once you have succeeded, return your partner's psychic body to its normal condition.

5. Should your partner ask you how you managed to win, go ahead and explain it. Better yet, show how it is done!

Note: This exercise was developed from an experience my then 15-year old daughter, Tanith, had in her high school lunch room. A large football "jock" sat down next to her and challenged her to an arm-wrestling session (with a bit more on his mind than that, I suspect!). Tanith immediately agreed, as long as he didn't mind lending some of his energy to her. She won, hands down! She also freaked the poor guy out rather badly. Needless to say, I couldn't argue with her logic that she had played fairly since she had asked him for his energy before she borrowed it. We did, however, talk about the necessity of explaining what happened in a way that wouldn't upset other people in the future.

The exercises that you have learned so far will help you become sensitive to what it feels like when the energy from your psychic body is being pulled away from you. Not everyone is nice enough to return the energy they take from you; therefore, you must learn to notice when and if something like that is going on in order to stop it.

Some people can (either knowingly or not) cut off a good-sized chunk of your psychic body and take it with them. This is a bit like being forced to give someone a pint or two of blood. Just as with blood, the substance of your psychic body will replenish itself over time, however you will feel decidedly weaker in all ways until this regeneration process is complete.

My own brother got a taste of this when I first showed him the four initial steps of Exercise 1. I was 21 at the time and he was a very active and athletic 16-year old. After I stretched out Bobby's psychic body and hung it up on one of the walls of the basement in my family's Connecticut home, he got so "weirded out" from experiencing the results that he wouldn't let me return his psychic body to its original condition. I finally left for my apartment. During the next week, my normally well-coordinated brother became an incredible "klutz" and was chronically tired. This eventually prompted my father (an orthopedic surgeon) to call me at the martial arts school where I worked and demand that I come home and undo whatever I had done to my brother. I, of course, did exactly that. I found that Bobby's psychic body had simply stayed stretched out because I had never unhooked it from the basement wall. I took care of it and my brother returned to normal almost immediately. Live and learn!!!

These exercises will also make you aware of both the mental switch that brings your psychic body in close to your physical body (contracting your energy), and the feeling that accompanies its use, so that it can only be used to your benefit. Finally, they will show you how to combine the psychic energy of others with your own to make your physical being stronger. Next, I will describe a series of exercises designed to strengthen your psychic/spiritual body.

EXERCISE 5
Centering

1. Sit down in a comfortable but preferably straight-backed chair. Set your feet flat on the floor. Allow your hands to rest quietly in your lap.

2. Close your eyes and listen to the sound of your own heartbeat.

3. Begin to tune your breathing to the beating of your heart. Breathe in to a four-beat; hold your breath in for a four-beat; exhale to a four-beat; and hold your breath out for a four-beat. This is known as four-fold breathing and should be done so that you breathe in and out through your nose while resting the tip of your tongue on the roof of your mouth slightly behind your front teeth.

4. Gradually slow down your breathing. Notice that your heart rate follows your breath now. Notice that your thinking processes begin to relax as well. Continue to slow down your breathing until you feel calm, relaxed, and develop a warm pleasant feeling in your belly. Once you achieve this, you will know what it feels like to be "centered."

EXERCISE 6
Grounding

1. Center yourself, following the steps in Exercise 5.

2. Forget about your heartbeat and place your attention on the soles of your feet. Allow a sensation of heat to build up under your arches.

3. Imagine that a beam of golden light extends from the bottom of each of your feet.

4. Each time you exhale imagine that these two beams of golden light extend farther from your feet and into the earth below you. (This may mean going through several floors and a building foundation first!) When your feet are firmly anchored in the earth, so that it seems it would be hard to move them if you tried, you have experienced the feeling of being "grounded."

Exercises 5 and 6 must be practiced until you can center and ground yourself in a few seconds, whether you are sitting, standing, or lying down (those beams of light can angle or curve down into the earth when necessary). The next exercise uses the sensitivity to your psychic body which was developed with Exercises 1 through 4, and the centering and grounding techniques learned in Exercises 5 and 6.

EXERCISE 7
Developing Your Psychic Shield

1. Center and ground yourself.

2. As you breathe in and out, pay attention to that part of your psychic body which extends beyond the

bounds of your physical body. With each inhalation of your breath, draw your psychic body/aura in closer to your physical body.

3. Continue Step 2 until your aura has been drawn into your physical body so much that its outer edges feel as if they are right at the level of your skin (the level at which it maximizes the strength it lends to the physical body and the level at which your physical, mental, and spiritual force maximally strengthens your psychic body).

4. Maintain this for no more than five minutes at first. You may gradually extend the time that you hold your psychic body at skin level until you can do this effortlessly and continuously if need be. (If you practice this exercise daily, you may increase the time by five minutes every three days.)

Note: The practice of this exercise will eventually create a shield that you will have to relax consciously when you wish to share your energy with others. The shield thus formed will be at least as effective as continuing to strongly assert that "no one may take your energy from you" and it has the eventual advantage of not having to be consciously maintained.

EXERCISE 8
Instant Psychic Shield

1. Center and ground yourself.

2. Practice Exercise 7, with the following addition. Each time you get to the point where the outer edges

of your psychic body/aura are level with your physical skin, visualize a protective symbol (cross, pentagram, hexagram, etc.) glowing brightly in the center of your forehead (your third-eye area).

3. After about six months of daily practice, just visualizing your protective symbol will have the effect of calling forth all the strength that you can muster into your psychic shield.

Exercises 7 and 8 will help you develop psychic shields which should protect you from most unconscious psychic vampires and the majority of conscious ones as well. Do remember that you have proved to yourself that you are capable of overwhelming the defenses of those with less experience. Eternal vigilance is the price of safety and freedom on all levels of living.

The next exercise is essential to good psychic hygiene.

EXERCISE 9

Draining Away Unneeded, Unwanted, and Just Plain "Bad Stuff" from Your Being

1. Center and ground yourself (do this lying down on your bed if you can).

2. While lying down on your bed (face up, arms at sides with palms up, legs slightly apart), imagine valves on the top of your head, in the centers of your palms, and on the centers of the soles of your feet.

3. Mentally open all five valves and tell yourself that everything that has attached itself to you from outside sources or from within yourself that is unneeded, unwanted, or just plain bad for you will flow from the top

of your head down through your body and out through your palms and feet over the next three minutes. Know that all of this unpleasant stuff will flow back to the source of everything to be purified and recycled.

4. Mentally close the valves on your palms and feet and open yourself up to the power of whatever God(s) you believe in (or simply universal energy if you prefer) for another three minutes so that you fill yourself up with clean, clear, and relaxing energy of the very best kind.

5. Mentally close the valve at the top of your head and enjoy.

Note: This same exercise can be done while standing in the shower and timed so that the shower washes out everything that needs to go; then as you air-dry for three minutes, you can draw in everything that is beneficial to you. (An overhead heat lamp would make a nice added touch to this process.)

The final basic exercise which I will present in this chapter has been described by many authors, including Israel Regardie and Alan Richardson. It is known as the Middle Pillar Exercise. This exercise is designed to help you absorb and make use of vitality from the world around you. As I explained earlier, humans are made up of several interpenetrating bodies, most of which are invisible to our five physical senses. Just as your physical body has organs designed to help you make use of the physical food you eat, your psychic body has organs designed to take in spiritual power and then to distribute and circulate this power where it can be used to your best advantage. When you gain control over this process through exercising it consciously, you can direct this power to bring about beneficial changes in your life and, potentially, the lives of others as well.

EXERCISE 10

The Middle Pillar Exercise (modified version)

1. Center and ground yourself in the sitting position.

2. Imagine a sphere of brilliant white light above the crown of your head. This sphere should be viewed as being active and abundantly alive with energy; it is your Spirit Center and the key to your true self. Vibrate the words *I Am* like a mantra, while maintaining this visualization.

3. After allowing your mind to rest here for five minutes, imagine that your Spirit Center sends out a shaft of white light down through your skull and brain, continuing until it stops at your throat and expands to form another sphere of brilliant white light. This is your Air Center. It is related to the powers associated with the planet Saturn. Keep this in mind as you focus your attention on this vital sphere.

4. After allowing your mind to rest here for five minutes, imagine that your Air Center sends out a shaft of white light down through your body until it reaches your solar plexus and expands into a sphere of brilliant white light. This is your Fire Center. It is related to the powers associated with the Sun. Experience its energy as you focus your attention on this active sphere.

5. After allowing your mind to rest here for five minutes, imagine that your Fire Center sends out a shaft of white light down through your body until it comes to your genital region, where it expands to form another sphere of brilliant white light. This is your Water Center. It is related to the powers associated with the Moon. Feel this energy as you focus your attention on this sphere.

6. After allowing your mind to rest here for five minutes, imagine that your Water Center sends out a shaft of white light down through your body until it reaches your feet, where it expands to form a final sphere of brilliant white light. This is your Earth Center. It is quite naturally related to the powers associated with the Earth and things such as food, clothing, and shelter. Dwell on this as you focus your attention on this sphere of solidity. Spend five minutes doing this.

7. Focus your attention on your Spirit Center and imagine it vigorously absorbing spiritual energy from the atmosphere around you. Exhale and visualize this energy flowing down the left side of your body. Inhale and visualize this same energy flowing under your feet and up the right side of your body to return to your Spirit Center. Notice that this energy is inside all of your bodies, both visible and invisible. Keep this visualization going until the energy has completed at least six full circuits.

8. Imagine that this energy flows from your Spirit Center down the front of your body to your feet as you exhale, and then flows under your feet and up the back of your body to return to your Spirit Center as you inhale. Continue this visualization until at least six full circuits have been completed.

9. Send your attention down to your Earth Center. This must be viewed as a vessel containing all power. Imagine that your Spirit Center is drawing this power up to it as you inhale in such a way that it fountains up out of your Spirit Center, and then, as you exhale, it falls down all around your body until it collects again in the vessel that your Earth Center has become. Visualize at least six of these fountaining circulations of power.

The total visual effect of this whole exercise will be what Don Juan of Carlos Castaneda's famous books would have called a scintillating, luminous egg of energy extending from the center of your being out to about an arm's length from the limits of your physical body. I have presented The Middle Pillar Exercise in a simplified form, however this will not detract from its usefulness in helping you pay attention to your psycho/spiritual organs and in strengthening your entire being. This exercise should be practiced daily. Remember: the stronger you are on all levels, the stronger will be your psychic shield when you need it!

It often helps to develop a daily routine when you are learning new skills. I would suggest that you begin each day with the Middle Pillar Exercise and end each day with the Draining Exercise. During the course of each day, you should find time to work on the other exercises presented in the first two chapters of this book. Keep a notebook to record the results of your efforts. An entry should be set up to look something like this:

Name:_____Date:_____

Time:_____Exercise:_____

Health (circle one): Excellent, Good, Fair, Poor

Explanatory comments on health:_____

_____

Weather Conditions:_____

Comments on Success of Exercise:_____

_____

CHAPTER 3

SPIRITUAL SURVIVAL TRAINING VERSUS PSYCHIC SELF-DEFENSE

A S I HAVE MENTIONED before, human beings have both physical and spiritual bodies. Both types of bodies must be cared for, since they obviously affect each other. As human beings, we also partake of both spiritual and animal natures which coincide with our spiritual and physical bodies. While we live on this Earth, we can choose to evolve spiritually through our earthly experiences, merely focus on the material desires of our animal existence, or do a little of both.

Many mystics and metaphysicians through the ages have taken the above information to indicate that humans as individuals are in all probability only *potentially* immortal. If they are correct, then each of us is obligated to insure our own spiritual survival by developing a meaningful relationship with Divinity.

Psychic self-defense does not insure the spiritual survival of your true self. It may, in fact, be dangerous even to study the more advanced technical aspects of this discipline before a meaningful working relationship with Divinity has been established. Practical training in any kind of self-defense requires the student to actively repel an actual attack. This means that the student of psychic self-defense will have to practice repelling "fail-safe" attacks in the beginning and work up to countering quite real assaults later in training.

Only after students have mastered the basics of flexibility (of mind), strength (of character), movement (of energy), and problem solving, should they seriously take up this training in its more advanced aspects. Ignoring this advice will only lead to injuries. Injuries directly related to precipitous behavior also often result in longterm debilitating fears bordering on paranoia, while experiencing success due more to dumb luck than to adequate training may generate a foolhardy and unjustified sense of self-confidence which will, in turn, lead to serious injuries later on for both students and their associates. Of course, the best self-defense technique (of any kind) for most people is to simply avoid dangerous situations through the application of common sense.

Some of us, however, cannot always avoid conflict by the very nature of our existence in this world. Just as firemen, soldiers, and policemen must face occasional danger because of the nature of their work, so must those of us who choose to actively and publicly use our psychic abilities. In this case, we must know how to defend ourselves. This includes taking special care to develop a working relationship with Divinity by whatever name(s) we know It.

Most spiritual traditions have two things in common. The first is a belief in some Supreme Being(s) who is (are) the source of our existence. The second is a stern warning to anyone who would dare to establish a true relationship with that Divinity. I have listed a few of these dire warnings below:

1. Narrow and rough is the road that leads to life (Jesus).[1]

2. The way is narrow, as narrow as a razor's edge (Hindu Scripture).[2]

---

[1] R. W. Funk and R. W. Hoovor, and the Jesus Seminar, *The Five Gospels* (New York: Macmillan, 1993), Matthew 7:14, p. 156.
[2] I cannot remember where this comes from.

3. No mere mortal may behold the greatest glory of the Holy Countenance and live (Western Inner Tradition).[3]

These statements leave no doubt that the Path toward an individual relationship with Divinity is difficult, dangerous, and potentially lethal. However, if you look for what is behind these "terribly serious" warnings, you will find certain evidence that the way is *not* impossible. As in any dangerous activity, the primary sources of peril are lack of adequate preparation and distraction.

In truth, the distractions are the most dangerous. For instance, I am sure that I am not the only esoteric-minded person who has grumbled that the demands of family, job, and community leave precious little time for less mundane pursuits. Come on; be honest with yourself! When was the last time that you used every bit of the time you had left over profitably pursuing your relationship with Divinity? I bet there were a good number of times when you simply decided to "rest" by watching the television and/or sipping your favorite beverage. Actually, there is nothing wrong with doing exactly that if you wish to, so long as you recognize that, in doing so, you also chose not to do quite a lot of other things when you had the chance.

The best resolution of the seemingly endless chain of mundane interruptions to our spiritual aspirations is acceptance of one very important fact:

> We are designed to live in the
> midst of both matter and spirit.

Again, if you look behind this statement, you realize that you are indeed capable of doing both at the same time. All of your activities, by their very nature, can be secular and spiritual simultaneously. The trick is in knowing how to accomplish this within the parameters of your daily life.

---

[3] Wm. G. Gray, *The Rite of Light* (Albany, NY: Privately published, 2nd ed., 1993), p. 14.

This is not at all a simple matter. In fact, I suggest that, in the beginning, it will be easier to separate the secular and spiritual aspects of your daily routine as much as possible, until you are very familiar with their feel. Most religious traditions would agree. There should be a time for physical and mental work, a time for family and friends (emotional exercise), and a time for spiritual work during the course of your daily life. The proportion of the day that is devoted to these activities will vary greatly from individual to individual. For those who dare to walk the razor's edge, it might be wise to devote roughly a tenth of the day pursuing a meaningful relationship with Divinity. The 2.4 hours this would entail could be spread out over the course of the day to include morning, midday, evening, and nightly devotions, exercises, and study, or the time could be collapsed into one or two longer periods of daily spiritual work. The rest of the day might be broken up into 9.6 hours which could be set aside for eating, sleeping, and physical exercise, 8 hours reserved for mental exertion (school, jobs, etc.), and 4 hours devoted to time spent with friends and family. This is merely a suggested schedule. You will have to assess your own lifestyle and needs before you are able to discipline yourself with a schedule of any type. The important thing is to order your life. Only then will it be possible to establish a feeling for the meaning behind each aspect of it. Of course, you must also remain flexible enough to accommodate whatever changes become necessary due to unforeseen circumstances. Once you can appreciate the secular and spiritual aspects of your life individually, then you can begin to integrate the two.

Let's review again the two main sources of danger to those who choose to walk the Razor's Edge:

Lack of adequate preparation

Specialized tasks require specialized knowledge and training. For instance, if you wish to become a medical doctor, you must be willing and able to complete very specialized educational requirements. Although not all professions require this much training, the majority require a fair amount beyond basic secondary schooling. Once fully trained, most professionals and technicians have the support of their peers and the respect of their communities. They also have the capacity to earn a living for themselves and their families.

Things are a bit different for those who seek an intimate relationship with Divinity. First of all, you simply cannot expect the support of society. While it is true that most people do not deny the existence of Divinity, they behave as if contact with It (personal or otherwise) is unnecessary to their way of life. Contemplation, meditation, and prayer are viewed as very nearly a waste of time. Even most religious communities fail to be particularly encouraging. After all, they are in the business of providing "go-betweens" for the masses of people who do not choose to seek out a personal relationship with the divine source of their existence.

The point is that, if you choose to walk the Razor's Edge, you cannot expect public support for your efforts. In fact, you may have to endure a fair amount of ostracism by "ordinary" people and, worse yet, the acclaim of genuine "crazies." The only way to avoid some of this is to heed the directive given to mystics and magicians of all ages: Be silent about your Quest, unless you are among like-minded people.

If, in spite of the problems already mentioned, you decide to Quest further along the Path toward a working relationship with Divinity, your problem of gaining adequate preparation will not disappear. There are almost no schools designed to train you for this highly individualistic pursuit. However, you can gain the knowledge and skills required by learning the techniques used by those Travelers of the Razor's Edge who have gone before you. Many of these have recorded their experiences in writing and some of these documents are still used to train seminarians.

You will undoubtedly have to depend mostly on yourself for your initial training. This can be dangerous. Contact with Divinity is likely to shake up your comfortable and familiar world fairly drastically. At this point, it might be wise to ask yourself if you have the objectivity and persistence to withstand the inevitable pressure to which you will be subjected.

One of the most difficult paradoxes you will face during the first stages of your training is the confusion created by the simultaneous requirements of developing enormous self-confidence and maintaining the virtue known as humility. The word humility derives from the Latin word *humus*, which means "earth." Being grounded in the truth is essential to your Quest. The inward journey Godward is filled with illusions (most of our own making). Without a firm anchor in the truth your Quest may lead only to self-destruction.

Distraction

Distractions are dangerous to those who would walk the Razor's Edge simply because the Way is narrow and a fall is likely to be debilitating. However, all of us are called to this Way at some time during our various lifetimes. The old saying, "Many are called, but few are chosen" might be more accurately stated as "All are called, but few at any given time have the perseverance to stay the course." The sacred journey is essential to your spiritual survival, but it is far better to leave it for the future than to risk a premature beginning.

Almost anything or anyone can be a distraction. The most powerful distractions, however, are the ones that play on your ego. Power, prestige, and politics are the three primary forces which serve to test your endurance. The temptation of power is self-evident. The trap of self-delusion goes hand-in-hand with it and the second source of distraction, the desire for prestige. As noted earlier, those who walk the Razor's Edge cannot expect the encouragement or acclaim of most other humans. Yet, that is often what they crave, is it not? It is far more comfortable to lay the responsibility for determining your true worth on others than it is to face the naked truth about yourself. The third source of distraction, politics, simply carries this one step further. I once heard a comedian giving a "fractured" definition of politics which was, nevertheless, quite appropriate. He said that the word "politics" derived from the Latin *poly*, meaning "many" and the English *ticks*, meaning "blood-sucking vermin." Therefore the "World of Politics" would be inhabited by "many blood-sucking vermin" and very little else!

HOW TO HUMBLY PREPARE
FOR THE SACRED JOURNEY

If you are going to leave the relative safety of the masses and transcend their religions, you must first learn to trust the Inner Guidance that will lead you to Divinity. The Gods did not stop speaking 2000 years ago, though in truth many of us have forgotten how to listen. The first step toward this goal requires a commitment to the type of daily living schedule that we spoke of earlier. Setting aside a dedicated period of time for physical, mental, emotional, and spiritual exercise will allow you to sort out the stimuli to which you are responding. For instance, if you are focusing on the physical requirements of your existence, you should be able to recognize the cues your body gives you concerning its needs. The same is true of all other aspects of yourself.

The next step is to keep a journal of daily events, feelings, observations, etc. This will help you to keep track of your progress. You should arrange your entries in the following manner:

Name:_____Date:_____Time:_____

Hour was dedicated to:_____

Weather Conditions:_____

Personal emotional/mental/physical state:_____

_____

Description of event/observation/feeling:_____

_____

Although it would be nice to make your journal recordings as close to the time of the events which caused them as possible, it will not always be convenient to do so. Usually the best that can be accomplished is to jot down a couple of notes to yourself which can be transferred to your journal later in the day. There are more journal forms printed on pages 101–108.

Many spiritual traditions have tried to regulate the spiritual devotions of their adherents. As stated earlier, establishing order in your life is the most important thing. One method designed to regulate spiritual exercises which I have found useful was suggested to me by Wm. G. Gray (I believe he published a version of this in the first volume of the Sangreal Sodality Series, *Western Inner Workings*). His idea was to split the 2-plus hours a day which you plan to devote to spiritual work into four distinct segments:

1. *Morning Meditation:* Take 5 to 10 minutes after you get up in the morning to concentrate on whatever spiritual studies you undertook the night before and allow any new information that may have come to you during your sleep

to surface from the depths of your consciousness. Make your journal entry concerning this.

2. *Midday Invocation:* Take time during the middle of the busiest part of your day to invoke intensely the Inner Power you hope is trying to guide you toward your best Pathway to Enlightenment.

3. *Evening Study:* Use the bulk of your time for reading and study of spiritually relevant topics.

4. *Nightly Quest:* Choose a topic to "sleep on" just before going to sleep. This is done so that the deeper awareness that can be contacted during your sleep may deal specifically with your needs.

After a month or two of following this schedule of spiritual exercises, you should begin to recognize the proddings that arise from your deepest levels of awareness as they surface throughout any and all parts of the day. These proddings may not always arrive at a "convenient time." However, it is always wise to pay close attention to them. You will come to recognize that indeed this Inner Guidance has always been available to you. In learning how to listen to it, you have taken a big step toward communicating with Divinity.

Patience will remain important, even after many years of experience with your Source of Inner Guidance. Even after you are confident that this communication can and does occur, it will not always be as plentiful or as comfortable as you might wish. There will be times when you wonder if you are actually getting anywhere at all. There will also be times when you feel overwhelmed by the direction in which you are being guided. As often as not, these times will coincide with inner proddings that demand your attention at all hours of the day and night, when you really would rather be doing something a bit more frivolous—like eating or sleeping, for instance!

If, from time to time, you find this as frustrating as do most of us, remember that communication is a two-way street. There is no reason in the world that you should not express the frustrations and difficulties you are having to the appropriate Source. After you ventilate your feelings, however, you should be prepared to go faithfully on about your daily business. Other people depend on you and, for their sakes, you must continue on as usual, even under the most trying of spiritual "black outs." Sooner or later (if you continue on with your spiritual exercises and don't give up), something will happen to restore your confidence in your Divine Guidance System and in Divinity Itself and you will have survived the single most difficult distraction of all—The Dark Night of the Soul.

CHAPTER 4

SIGNS OF PSYCHIC DISTURBANCE AND PSYCHIC FIRST AID

D ION FORTUNE ONCE SAID, "We live in the midst of invisible *forces* whose effects alone we perceive.... We move among invisible *forms* whose actions are often not perceived by us even if we are profoundly affected by them."[1] These two statements, plus the exercises I have introduced in this book so far, will lead you to believe (and rightly so) that it would be well to know the physical symptoms associated with a psychic body which has become unbalanced regardless of the cause. Here is a list of the most common of these symptoms:

1. A feeling of weight pressing down on your chest while you are asleep or dreaming.

2. A continuous and intensifying sense of oppression or fear. (Note: Those who are sensitive will feel this sensation before anything actually goes wrong. Consider it as part of your intuitive "early warning system.")

3. Nervous exhaustion or wasting way to "skin and bone" when there is no observable physical cause or disease process.

---

[1] Dion Fortune, *Psychic Self-Defense* (York Beach, ME: Samuel Weiser, 1992), p. 25. Italics mine.

4. Being terrified of going to sleep.

5. Dreaming of fighting with something and waking up with bruises in all the "right" places. (This is known as the Phenomenon of Repercussion.)

6. Obnoxious odors that come and go with no apparent physical cause. (These odors will be noticed by anyone who is around when they are present. These are not the phantom odors associated with some types of psychosis.)

7. Seeing odd footprints that come from no particular place and just stop without seeming to go to any particular destination.

8. Inexplicable outbreaks of fire. (This is often associated with elemental activity.)

9. Poltergeist activity.

10. Inexplicable precipitations of slime or powdery substances.

Most people become susceptible to psychic interference in their lives due to three different types of suggestion:

1. autosuggestion;

2. conscious suggestion;

3. hypnotic suggestion.

Autosuggestion originates with the self. Conscious suggestion comes from someone other than yourself through the use of the spoken or written word. Hypnotic suggestion enters the subconscious mind directly through an in-person rapport with the subject, sleep teaching, or telepathic suggestion.

All types of suggestion affect the subconscious mind of an individual. The idea is to influence or by-pass the conscious mind so that it cannot block the suggestion to the subconscious mind. The subconscious mind acts like a good soldier and simply does what it is told to do. This is true whether the "teller" is your built-in biological programming which keeps you breathing, your blood flowing, etc., your conscious mind, or someone outside of yourself.

Technically speaking, suggestion of any kind is not necessarily a bad thing. You can use autosuggestion (also known as self-hypnosis) to correct a bad habit or relieve pain. You can even ask someone else to help you to achieve these worthy goals by the use of conscious (mind-to-mind) suggestion or hypnosis. It is only when suggestions that are not in your best interest are sent without your conscious knowledge and consent that things can get sticky.

Since all types of suggestion aim at influencing the subconscious mind, it is well worth knowing how that part of you works. Your subconscious mind is more primitive in origin and function than your conscious mind. It is associated with your basic "animal" instincts. Your subconscious mind communicates through the use of symbols. Therefore, your conscious mind must be trained to recognize and utilize the same symbols that your subconscious mind uses if you wish to use autosuggestion constructively. Please note that words are symbols, just as visual images are symbols. Do not despair of working with your subconscious programming if you happen to be one of those people whose primary sense is not sight. In fact, almost anything can be a symbol. Depending on what you use, you may need to train your subconscious mind to understand the symbols that you consciously choose to use in your communication with it. This is exactly what is done when you learn to use a psychic tool like tarot cards.

One of the easier ways to affect your subconscious mind or that of another is to make a mental or verbal picture of what needs to be done. This picture should be concentrated upon repeatedly until your subconscious mind takes it up as its own and acts upon it.

This procedure is most effective when your suggestion reinforces or stimulates the ideas or commands already present in your subconscious mind. Obviously you are aiming at creating a mental atmosphere around yourself or whomever you intend to influence which will elicit a sympathetic mental and/or emotional response in yourself or your subject. Once this is accomplished, you have opened the door to further and more direct telepathic suggestions. Should you be under psychic attack, this is the critical point. Up until this point, you, as the defender, have the advantage. *After this point the attacker is in charge!*

There are two primary points of entry into the subconscious mind: the survival instincts of self-preservation and reproduction. Direct hypnotic appeals made to identify with either of these instincts virtually guarantee success. However, should attacks be aimed at these instinctual processes, the risk of "backfire" is also very high. An attacker must think about his victim to create an atmosphere around him. This atmosphere works through the attacker rather than directly on the victim/defender. If the victim fails to react with fear or desire, the atmosphere created by the attacker is going to find its outlet with the attacker rather than the victim.

The victim of a psychic disturbance or attack needs three basic services to be performed for him:

1. Contact with the source of the attack or disturbance must be cut off.

2. The psychic atmosphere around the victim must be purified.

3. The victim's aura must be strengthened and/or repaired.

The order in which these services are performed is normally controlled by the specific circumstances in which the victim is found.

Contact can often be cut between the source of the disturbance and the victim by having the victim move, taking nothing with him or her. Obviously this is easier said than done for most people. A somewhat easier solution would be to have the victim temporarily move to a friend's home or safehouse, taking only the bare necessities—and these should be purified before leaving the original environment. This will buy time for the victim in which the other services may be performed.

Temporary defenses may be set up to allow for the purification of the victim's environment. This is normally accomplished by purifying the victim's home with Earth and Water (Blessed and Consecrated Salt Water) and sealing it with Fire and Air (Blessed and Consecrated Incense).

The following are formulas for blessing and consecrating the elements of Earth and Water which I have found useful. They were devised by Wm. G. Gray for use in his Rite of Light.[2] Any other suitable formula may, of course, be used. The important thing is that the formula feel potent to you each and every time you use it.

SALT:

Creature of salt, thou faithful friend of man,
Be unto us a practical and potent means of
Preserving good from evil.

[Make the sign of the Cosmic Cross using your right hand in the sign of benediction while saying:]

---

[2] Wm. G. Gray, *The Rite of Light* (Albany, NY: Privately published, 1993), pp. 15–16.

In the Name of the Wisdom [touch forehead],
And of the Love [touch heart],
And of the Justice [touch right shoulder],
And of the Infinite Mercy [touch left shoulder],
Of the One Eternal Spirit [circle face],
Amen [touch upper lip just under nose].

SALT IN WATER [right hand over water]:

May our bodies, minds, and souls forever be preserved
from all corruption by the action of pure spiritual Light,
diffusing through us as this salt dissolves in water, sym-
bolizing our intentions of expelling evils from us by our
uttermost exertions.

WATER:

O Infinite Divinity, from whose eternal ocean every single soul emerges into Life, we, thy scattered drops, salute
thee through our symbol of this water. Bless thou thine
element of Life in us, so that our inner seed of spiritual
Light may germinate and grow to its full glory.

In the Name of the Wisdom [touch forehead],
And of the Love [touch heart],
And of the Justice [touch right shoulder],
And of the Infinite Mercy [touch left shoulder],
Of the One Eternal Spirit [circle face],
Amen [touch upper lip just under nose].

Once the elements of Water and Earth have been blessed
and consecrated, they should be taken throughout the victim's home and belongings, and liberally sprinkled with
the intention of purifying his or her environment.

The following formulas for the blessing and consecration of Fire and Air come from the works of Paul Huson

and Wm. G. Gray.[3] Again, if you have or find others that
work better for you, by all means use them.

LIGHT CHARCOAL AND ADD GRANULATED INCENSE OR USE JOSS STICK:

**May our thoughts and prayers on Earth create an atmos-
phere as welcome to Divinity within our midst as the de-
lightful fragrance from the precious flowers of paradise
itself** [right hand over incense smoke].

**Creatures of Fire and Air, this charge I lay,
No phantom in thy presence stay.
Hear my words addressed to thee
And as my will,
So mote it be!**

In the Name of the Wisdom [touch forehead],
And of the Love [touch heart],
And of the Justice [touch right shoulder],
And of the Infinite Mercy [touch left shoulder],
Of the One Eternal Spirit [circle face],
Amen [touch upper lip just under nose].

After the elements of Fire and Air have been blessed and
consecrated, the incense should be taken through the victim's home and fanned into all nooks and crannies and
onto all belongings, to seal the environment against further
intrusion.

Strengthening the victim's aura/psychic body can be
accomplished in a number of ways. First and foremost he
or she should be taken to a doctor for a full physical exami-

---

[3] The first four lines are from *Rite of Light*, by Wm. G. Gray (page 7) and
the second part is adapted from Paul Huson, *Mastering Witchcraft* (New
York: G.P. Putnam's Sons/Perigee Books, 1980), p. 49.

nation. Anything that a medical doctor can do to strengthen the physical body of a victim of psychic disturbance adds to that person's stamina and endurance, which can be critical factors in defense. Sleeping pills should be avoided if possible. Artificially deepened sleep can leave people much more vulnerable to psychic attack during sleep than they would be normally. If a doctor insists that a victim who has been deprived of sleep must get some rest, then it will be necessary for someone with the appropriate knowledge to safeguard the victim's sleep. Sunlight and exercise will strengthen the aura. However, a victim of psychic disturbance should avoid going to areas of high elemental strength, such as the ocean, high mountains, and the wilderness. Group exercises and games are more appropriate to such a victim than are solitary walks, which may open the pathways to fear and paranoia. Keeping the bowels flowing smoothly will also help. Constipation can create septic focal points which may be taken advantage of by an attacker.

Diet is also important to the victim of a psychic disturbance and/or attack. A vegetarian or vegan diet is not a good idea for someone in a weakened psychic condition. These diets tend to make people more, rather than less, sensitive to the invisible realms. A balanced diet which is low in sugar content, yet which emphasizes the foods normally available from the land and surroundings of the victim's home, is the best bet when your object is to build physical and psychic strength and endurance. Remember that the condition of the physical body will affect the psychic body just as the condition of the psychic body affects physical functions.

Finally, there are a number of different substances that can affect the strength of anyone's aura. Tobacco is not just bad for your lungs. It will actually weaken your psychic body. Garnets, on the other hand will strengthen your psychic body. Try Exercise 2 (page 10), but instead of stretching your partner's aura out, have your partner hold a closed box or package of cigarettes in the left hand; then do the second strength test. The results should be dramatic. In fact, even if your partner has become accomplished at keeping his or her aura pulled in close to the physical body, just holding the cigarettes should cause significant weakness. Imagine what habitual smokers do to themselves! Now try this same exercise, but substitute a garnet or two for the box of cigarettes. Notice that your partner seems considerably stronger while in contact with this stone.

All substances have their own particular energy signatures. Some work well with us and some do not. Experiment with different foods, metals, stones, etc. Some of these substances will have effects on you that are idiosyncratic. Note which ones these are. For those of you who are addicted to tobacco products, try the exercise suggested earlier in this paragraph with the box of cigarettes. Then try it again, having your partner hold both the cigarettes and a garnet or two. You should notice that the garnets neutralize the effect of the cigarettes on the psychic and physical body and may even overcome their effect so that your partner appears to be stronger than at the beginning of the exercise. Table 1 (page 42) gives some substances and their usual beneficial effects on the psychic body. Remember to test these for yourself, since some people (due to their specific make-up) react differently to individual stimuli.

Psychic attacks affect a victim through the psychic centers (Spirit—above the crown of the head; Air—throat; Fire—solar plexus; Water—genital region; and Earth—feet). If these psychic centers can be closed off temporarily, the victim of psychic disturbance or attack will gain relief. The most vulnerable psychic centers are Spirit, Air, Fire, and Water. If the blood can be drawn away from these centers through hot baths, soaking the feet in hot mustard and water, or keeping the belly full by eating every two hours, relief from psychic distress is almost certain. A hot water

Table 1. The Effects of Substances on the Psychic Body.*

SUBSTANCE	USUAL EFFECT ON THE PSYCHIC BODY
Agate (banded)	Restores vigor.
Adventurine	Strengthens sight on all levels.
Bloodstone (Green Chalcedony flecked with red spots)	Increases strength; helps to heal.
Carnelian	Dispels depression on all levels.
Garnet	Enhances strength on all levels.
Basil	Helps create rapport between people; Repels evil influences.
Blueberry	Helps strengthen all bodies; Repels psychic disturbance/attack.
Carnations	When placed in one's room, these flowers help heal and build strength.

*For a more extensive list of this variety see *Cunningham's Encyclopedia of Magical Herbs*, *Cunningham's Encyclopedia of Crystal, Gem and Metal Magic*, and *The Magic in Food*, all by Scott Cunningham.)

bottle applied with pressure to the Fire Center is also helpful. If the victim must be out and about, a firm pad held in place over the solar plexus with a belt or girdle will do the trick.

The above is essentially a quick course in First Aid for victims of psychic disturbance or attack. Although the procedures outlined here are temporary by nature, they are often enough. If the disturbance originates within the victim, these aids will buy time to get the situation under control. If it originates from some outside source, you must realize that sustained psychic attack takes vast quantities of both time and energy. If you are not easy prey, the attacker will move on in search of easier pickings.

NOTE: *Anyone who is experiencing either psychic disturbance or attack should avoid any practices designed to open them up psychically/spiritually. These people should be advised to lead conservative and mundane lives for at least a year and a day before beginning any type of spiritual, psychic, or metaphysical exercise.*

CHAPTER 5

THE BEST DEFENSE
IS A GOOD OFFENSE

THOSE OF US WHO ARE called to serve as Guardians of the Light within this world need to know how to protect ourselves, our loved ones, and those who come to us in need of help. Because of our vocation, we must seek training beyond what is necessary for the average person who has just begun to deal with the invisible forces and forms which affect their lives. Although I do not propose to offer a full course of this type of training in this particular volume, I am making available what amounts to "Basic Training for a Spiritual Warrior."

Warriors are men and women who dedicate themselves to the promotion, preservation, and protection of a particular Cause. Normally a Cause of sufficient worth to warrant the development of a Warrior Tradition has a recognizable Spiritual Presence and/or Power behind it. When this Cause is pro-human in orientation, the duty of the Warrior is to do Good and avert Evil. Therefore, choosing the Path of the Warrior under these conditions requires a very personal recognition of the laws of polarity which govern earthly existence, and an appreciation of these laws for what they really are.

A Spiritual Warrior must know, understand, and deal with both Good and Evil. Wm. G. Gray often said to me:

> [Anyone] who is intent on growth and spiritual evolution toward Divinity is duty bound to under-

stand that which is either Wrong or Evil, control this by the use of severe measures, and avert it by adhering to an honorable lifestyle while at the same time seeking the wisdom to know that which is Right or Good, extend this by compassion and consolidate it through personal victories.[1]

The seeking of spiritual guidance and the practice of creating a safe space where you and The Powers That Be can meet and communicate is essential to the life of a Spiritual Warrior. Below, you will find an adaptation of what is known as the Lesser Banishing Ritual of the Pentagram (originally of Golden Dawn fame) that is ideally suited to both these purposes. As I have adapted this rite to better fit my spiritual tradition,[2] so should you be able to do if the need arises.

Lesser Banishing Ritual of the Pentagram
(Modified Version)

CENTER: COSMIC CROSS

In the Name of [with the first two fingers of the right hand]
The Wisdom [touch forehead],
And of the Love [touch heart);
And of the Justice [touch right shoulder],
And of the Infinite Mercy [touch left shoulder]
Of the One Eternal Spirit [circle face],
Amen [touch upper lip just under nose].

---

[1] This is echoed in his *Tree of Evil* (York Beach, ME: Samuel Weiser, 1984), p. 5.
[2] Adapted from Israel Regardie, *The Complete Golden Dawn System of Magic* (Phoenix, AZ: New Falcon, 1987), pp. 68–70.

EAST:

[With a Sword, draw the Banishing Pentagram of Earth in the air before you (see figure 5, page 48). Exhale on downward strokes. Inhale on upward strokes. Hold your breath on horizontal strokes. Stab the center of this Pentagram with your sword and vibrate]:

YOD-HE-VAU-HE

[YHVH—this means simply "the Sound that began Creation, The Cosmic Shout or Laugh." Once the Pentagram is glowing with power, circle to the South with your sword extended in front of you so that it draws a quarter of the magic circle in power.]

SOUTH:

Repeat what was done in the East, except that this Pentagram must be charged with the vibrated word:

ADONAI

[ADNI—this means "Lord." Inscribe the circle from South to West as you did before from East to South.]

WEST:

Repeat what was done in the South, except that this Pentagram must be charged with the vibrated word:

EHEIEH

[EHIH—this means "The Breath of Life." Inscribe the circle from West to North as you did before from South to West.]

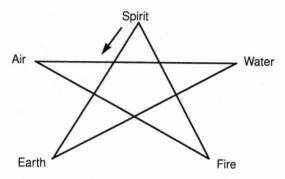

Figure 5. Banishing Pentagram of Earth.

NORTH:

[Repeat what was done in the West, except that this Pentagram must be charged with the vibrated word]:

AGLA

[This "name" is composed of the first letters of each word in a phrase which is descriptive of Divinity. Inscribe the circle from North to East as you did before from West to North. Return to Center.]

CENTER:

[Stand in Pentagram (Star of Mankind) position, facing East and chant]:

Before me, Raphael,
Behind me, Gabriel,
On my right hand, Michael,
On my left hand, Auriel,
About me flame the Pentagrams,
Above me shines the six-rayed star (Hexagram/Star of God).

Visualize yourself standing on and grounded by a Black Cube completely encompassed by sacred and protected space and say:

May the Light Descend.

[Visualize the Light coming from the Star of God down through your crown to fill your entire being and radiate out to fill the Magical Sphere you have constructed.]

NOTE: Meditation, Petitions for Guidance or help, Magical Work, or nothing at all may be done at this point. End this ritual with the Cosmic Cross and use the Banishing Ritual of the Pentagram of Earth, remembering to draw back into yourself in whispers the Divine Names with which you charged each Pentagram. Visualize yourself as reeling in (as in fishing) the Circle as you do this. You could also see yourself drawing the aura back into yourself.

The symbol of the Spiritual Warrior's service to both Divinity and Humanity is the Sword and the password is "Peace." You acknowledge that your peace can only be maintained through strength, hence you are willing to learn both how to defend and how to destroy.

Whether actual or symbolic, a Spiritual Warrior's Sword should only be drawn in the name of the Cause served, or at the word of a superior who is willing to take the responsibility of command. You must never draw your Sword for use in fighting personal quarrels. "He who fights a private battle, fights alone." However, if the need to draw your Sword does arise, you must be prepared to fight until the battle is won.

The Sword of the Spiritual Warrior is claimed by your own will and actions. This sword is normally sought through initiation. Wm. G. Gray created what is one of the more impressive Sword Initiations I have ever come across. While this work has not previously been published, it is now time for the world to have access to this particular rite so that those who will may make use of it. Some basic knowledge of the Qabalah is helpful in understanding the symbolism used in this ritual. Please feel free to adapt this initiation as needed to fit your own spiritual tradition.

Gaining the Sword
[by Wm. G. Gray]

Participants in this ritual

> The Candidate;
> The Questioner (Guide of Souls);
> The Preceptor (Master of Ceremonies);
> The Pontifex (Priest or Priestess).

Preparations

After due preparation, when the Temple is opened and set up with covered Sword and Stone upon the altar, and the center of the floor is inscribed with a five-foot pentacle and pentagram, with all appropriate adjuncts in their proper place, the Candidate is admitted after proper knocks and challenge at the Portals.

The Ritual

Candidate: [Knocks 5 times: *, *, *, *.]

Questioner: **Who seeks?**

Candidate: **One who would serve with an appointed Sword.**

Questioner: **What is the Word of Entrance?**

Candidate: **Peace with Strength proclaimed through Wisdom.**

Preceptor: **Admit with caution and due guard.**

[Candidate enters between a lighted torch and naked sword, with stones below the feet making entry difficult.]

Preceptor: **We bid you welcome and give greetings gladly unto all preservers of our Peace. What is your present purpose with us?**

Candidate: **I would earn a Sword with which alone that Peace can be carefully kept.**

Preceptor: **What is a Sword?**

Candidate: **A defender or destroyer, as it is directed.**

Preceptor: **How does it defend?**

Candidate: **By guard and parry.**

Preceptor: **How does it destroy?**

Candidate: **By point and edge.**

Preceptor: **How is it held in honor?**

Candidate: **In salutation.**

Preceptor: **How in dishonor?**

Candidate: **Broken.**

Preceptor: **Bear in mind that, when entering this place, you passed between a fiery sword upon a stony way. That** teaches you the perils of this Office. Above your head alone lay no impediment. That should show you where to look for guidance from the hands of Heaven. A sword you seek; a sword you seem to have already. What in yourself is most like unto a sword?

Candidate: [prompted] **My tongue.**

Preceptor: **Your tongue.** A human tongue is like unto a sword in that it has a point, two edges, and may move according to the will of whosoever wields it. It can defend or injure, save or lose human lives, and, though it be but inches long and speak for seconds, it can slay tall men for many years. Use your tongue as if it were a sword, and your sword as if it were a tongue. Guard particularly what you say when you reply to others. Parry that with which you cannot deal directly otherwise, so that no hurt will come to either side. Let your speech have edge, that it may cut confusing and unnecessary verbiage, yet give your words point that they may penetrate and make their mark upon their hearer's consciousness, even as the point of this my sword makes you aware of it at this moment.

[The Preceptor prods gently at the Candidate's right shoulder.]

It is the point of every uttered word wherein its highest value lies. In skilled hands, point must win from edge in every argument. Remember always your allegiance to the Sovereign Commander of our Universe and the appointed Great Ones unto whom our dedicated duty lies. Acknowledge with uplifted sword the sign of your companionship with all our kindred company. Give salutations unto those deserving them, and let your speech be as your sword—bright, polished, keenly flexible, and always pointed purposefully. Finally, let your tongue be never serpent's—poisonous and deadly. So keep yours single, clean, and always ready to defend the cause of Justice and Eternal Truth. Remember, above all, these ancient words: "In speech are many pitfalls, but in Silence—None." When should a sword be drawn?

Candidate: At the word of a commander who must authorize its use.

Preceptor: When should it *not* be drawn?

Candidate: For personal aggression in a private quarrel.

Preceptor: Now hear this instruction. True soldiers make no use of arms in their own name, but only in the name of the cause which they must serve. The Sword of the Wise must only be unsheathed and used in service of the Group or Company to which is owed allegiance. Only in salutes of honor may an individual uplift the sword, except in justifiable defense of integrity. Attack is utterly forbidden unless so ordered by superior officers who take upon themselves the full responsibility for such an action. Remember that those who fight private battles fight alone. Whosoever liveth by the sword is also liable thereby to perish. Therefore draw not your sword without a proper reason, neither sheathe it till that purpose be accomplished. Is this fully understood?

Candidate: It is.

Preceptor: Where hangs the sword upon the Holy Tree of Life?

Candidate: At the Fifth Station. Fear, Justice, and Requital.

Preceptor: Why the fifth?

Candidate: **Because, before the sword is drawn, the first four Principles apply.**

Preceptor: **What are those principles?**

Candidate: **The Summative Spirit, Wisdom, Understanding, and Mercy.**

Preceptor: **Remember, then, not to use the sword unless those principles are first involved and duly honored. Be a blessing bidden on us for that purpose.**

Pontifex: **O Strictest Spirit of Severity and Strength, thou Holy Judge of infinite integrity whose justice is the equalizer of existence, and whose Divine decision may not ever be denied, be thou our discipline and deal with us according to our due deserts, so that we may discharge our debts incurred to destiny. Thou art the eternal enemy of evil by whom all wrongs will surely be requited and all corruption cleansed throughout our Cosmos. Purge us, we pray, from every pestilence which would prevent our progress on our pathways to Perfection.**

O thou the fifth upon the Holy Tree of Life, Gevurah the strong severe One, thou in whom both Fear and Reason are combined to form Respect, thou whose Intelligence is termed the Radical, become thou rooted likewise in ourselves so that we may stand securely rooted also in thy strength and thus defend ourselves against all dangers.

Thou that hast the Holy Name of Elohim Gibor, the Lord of Battles, accept thou us as willing warriors within thy hosts since we would also serve as soldiers acting under thy command and do our duty faithfully while fighting in thy Cause. May we always understand thine orders and obey them without flinching. Be thou our absolute author-

ity within the world of Archetypes and bring us all to brotherhood beneath the standard of thine orange banner.

O great Archangel Khamael, thou the Burning One, be thou to us the beacon of our watchfire in the world which is creative. Injure not our true identities, but burn that in us which is dross and fit for nothing save destruction. Temper us within the Flame of Truth, and sanctify us with the scarlet redness of thy searching rays.

O Holy Seraphim, thou angels of the fiery serpentine appearance, remove all rashness, rage, and irritations from us whenever these result in our vengeful inclinations. Give us instead calm courage to combat the worst within us and be fellow fighters in the world of our formation.

Liberate us from all dangers of entanglement, even as the cleansing fumes of sulfur free us from infections borne by battles, and be thy brilliant scarlet banner unto us a badge of highest honor.

Thou who art named Madim, otherwise called Mars within this world of matter, spare us from savagery and stupid strife. Let not our world be ravaged and laid waste by wars. Show each one of us instead how we may find and fight the enemy, not in each other, but each one of us within ourselves. Be thy black and red a point of rally for us on the battlefield between our births and deaths.

O thou whose symbol is the sword and scourge, be unto us a surgeon not a slayer. Rule our right arms with resolution so we may conduct ourselves with courage on our fields of inner conflict and succeed in every struggle against evil on this earth and everywhere within existence. So mote this be, AMEN.

Preceptor: It is written that to whom you entrust a

sword you also entrust your life. Having due regard toward the safety of our Order and this company thereof, together with our good repute and our responsibility thereto, you are required to make this promise on your word of honor ere the sword may pass from us to you Attend it carefully.

I, _____, promise on and in the peril of my honor and my faith that I will never use my weapon of the Sword in this or any world against my spiritual brethren and Craft Companions, excepting under highest orders fully understood from constituted officers of superior rank who take upon themselves the full responsibility for such a lamentable action. In other matters, let the common code of honorable conduct bind me. As I shall use my weapon of the Sword, so be the Sword of Heaven directed to myself. Between my brethren and I, be peace profound forevermore. So may this be, Amen.

Are you willing to so promise?

Candidate: I am.

Preceptor: [Preceptor proffers his own sword hilt first.] Then place your right hand on the hilt of this true sword and so repeat your promise, remembering that the witnesses who hear your words have done so from their inmost souls.

[Here the Oath is administered phrase by phrase. At the end the Preceptor says:]

Companions of this company, you have heard these uttered words and formed a judgment of them in your hearts. How say you thereto? Shall this sword be given, yea or nay? Let whosoever is against this gift stand forth and be prepared for due and proper conflict of dispute

upon this issue here and now, according to the olden custom. Who says yea?

Pro faction: **I do.**

Preceptor: **And who says Nay?**

Anti faction: **I do.**

[Here a conventional dispute is arranged in some fashion
so that the Candidate comes out satisfactorily, whereupon
the Preceptor says:]

Preceptor: **Right well are you acquitted at the hands of
Gods and men alike. Receive our acclamation and accord.**

ALL: `IPI HU RA HE. IPI. HU. RA. HE. IPI HU RA HE.

Preceptor: **Yet not from our unworthy hands may you receive your sword. Of your own will and actions must you
claim it in the ancient way. Attend and understand. What
are you now shown?**

[The altar is uncovered.]

Candidate: **A Sword and Stone.**

Preceptor: **What is the significance thereof?**

Candidate: **The stone is a symbol of our Mother Earth beneath our feet, who one day will repose above our heads.**

Preceptor: **What is stone to steel?**

Candidate: **A sharpener.**

Preceptor: **What is steel to stone?**

Candidate: **A striker forth of fire.**

Preceptor: **What is the value of a sword?**

Candidate: **Its sharpness.**

Preceptor: **Remember then. Because of stone, our sword is sharpened, and from stone the sword produces our First Father—Fire. Here, therefore, you perceive our Primal Parents as Almighty Father-Mother. Mark this mystery well and meditate thereon. Even as a sword is sharpened on the stone, so may your faculties be keener, and so by the fire may you find enlightenment upon your path to Peace. First, however, hear the destiny that is pronounced upon the Sword and Stone: WHOSO DARES UPLIFT THE SWORD IN SEPARATION FROM THE STONE INVOKES THE CHALLENGE OF THE MIGHTIEST GODS THEMSELVES. The curse of Cain descended on those who first took iron from the Earth and fashioned it into their weapons aimed against all other human lives. None shall escape this curse excepting they that know and speak the Word of Liberation. Have you this word? What is it? Proclaim it forth aloud or take the consequences of an ill-timed silence.**

[The Preceptor menaces the Candidate with his own sword.]

Candidate: [prompted] **LOVE**

[The threat is removed].

Preceptor: **The Gods themselves that word obey. Take up your sword in that most Blessed Name. Sharpen it four times upon the stone. Uplift it in salute to the Immortal Ones, and say: IN THIS SIGN I SEEK TO SERVE.**

[This is done.]

Preceptor: **Carry Sword. You have heard it said that whatsoever gift that cuts should be exchanged against a coin or some small token to prevent misfortune following. This custom must be here observed. Place a little coin upon the stone in payment for the sword. Having no such thing upon you, borrow one from an obliging brother or sister soldier for this purpose.**

[This is done.]

From this, observe how we lift the sword in debt to one another. As you yourself have been assisted, so help all worthy comrades in their times of need. There will be times when you must fight the battles of one weaker than yourself, and there will be moments when you must invoke the aid of those who are more powerful than yourself. Remember that we fight together in common Cause. Even as you gained much for a small offering, so give much in return for small spiritual recompense. Such circumstances interchange, and you will be the gainer in each case. Answer truly. Where did you obtain that Sword?

Candidate: **From the Earth.**

Preceptor: **What forged the blade?**

Candidate: **Fire.**

Preceptor: **What blew the fire?**

Candidate: **Air.**

Preceptor: **What tempered the steel?**

Candidate: **Water.**

Preceptor: **What Craft is this?**

Candidate: **The Craft of Tubal-Cain.**

Preceptor: **Let the Olden Ones be honored with their own traditional salute.**

[Here there is hammering on an anvil, followed by an explosion.]

ALL: **HAIL TO THOSE OF OLDEN TIMES WHO LEARNED AND HANDED DOWN TO US THE USAGES OF OUR METALLIC ELEMENTS. IN TRUTH WE WILL FORGE ON.**

Preceptor: **Of the Earth are all things made, and by Their hallowed means are consecrated our especial symbols of the magic arts. It is the custom, from most ancient times, to name and dedicate a sword so used. How will you name this new-claimed Sword of yours?**

Candidate: _____.

Perceptor: _____, **in that Name we therefore act. Lay your sword upon that altar and stand by.**

[The Candidate does so.]

Pontifex: **Hear us, O thou sole, supreme, and incomparable Master-Craftsman of Creation, in whose name is made and manifested everything within existence or that ever will exist. We, thine instruments, acknowledging the insufficiency of our own means in action, here admit our use of artifice and symbol to assist us in the conduct and continuance of these Most Holy Mysteries. We, the yet** imperfect work of thine all-perfect hands, present to thee this token of our earthly skills made solely for our usage in thy Name.

[Elevates Sword briefly.]

Blessed be it to us and us to it. Sanctify for us this sword and charge it with thy fullest power so that it will protect us faithfully in thy most Perfect Peace.

[Breathes on it.]

By the Blessed Breath of Life which animates and vivifies all living things, become to us a sacred symbol of that Spirit which survives the strongest struggles.

[Pontifex passes the sword through a flame.]

By the fire of Love in which Truth must be tried and tempered, be thou a sure defense against the snares of all delusions formed by malice or from darkness in our minds.

[Pontifex applies lustral water to sword.]

By the waters of Compassion, which would spare us suffering, be thou like unto a welcome lancet, saving souls from sickness and approaching evils.

[Pontifex applies ashes or earth to sword.]

By the Earth in which we here and now exist, be thou unto us a practical and potent means whereby we serve the Holy Cause in which we are applied against all opposition.

[Pontifex magnetizes the sword with a magnet.]

By the poised polarity of principles, be thou the silent sign of ordered opposition. Attract thou Good; repel thou Evil. Be thou a lodestone for spiritual seekers and a perfect pointer of our proper way within this world.

[Pontifex signs sword with Holy Oil.]

Be thou sealed with sanctity, anointed and controlled by conscience, set apart from others of thy kind and dedicated to thy special duties. In the name of ELOHIM GIBOR, receive the contact of thy consecration. By the light of KHAMAEL, accept this mark of thine activity. Through the ordered office of the SERAPHIM, take thou this sign of service. O Princes of the Holy Presence, pour into this and us thy full protective power. Glory be to thee, O MICHAEL, Leader of the Hosts of Light; bless thou this enterprise and this its outcome. Send down, we pray, a guardian angel who will serve with us in this, A Sword, now duly dedicated to the Mysteries of Right and Light.

Be the name of _____ a point of contact set between our inner and outer worlds. Come thou forth, O holy hidden one who will accept this name as thy responsibility for service in this ancient art. Take up this Sword and, whenever that especial name of _____ is uttered urgently, stand ever at the side of _____ [Candidate's name] when perils press or should there be occasion for another service. We thank thee and would ask no more of thee or this companion than the olden charge: DO THOU THY DUTY.

[Pontifex presents Sword to the Candidate.]

Raise thou thy Sword on high and say: "O Highest One of all, behold and bless this Sword of mine, _____."

[Candidate does so.]

Now point to the depths and say: "All ye that live in Earth, behold and bless this Sword of mine, _____."

[Candidate does so.]

Now point it to the East and say: "Thou Holy Ones appointed to the East, behold and bless this Sword of mine, _____."

[Candidate does so.]

Now to the South and say: "Thou Holy Ones appointed to the South, behold and bless this Sword of mine, _____."

[Candidate does so.]

Now to the West and say: "Thou Holy Ones appointed to the West, behold and bless this Sword of mine, _____."

[Candidate does so.]

Now to the North and say: "Thou Holy Ones appointed to the North, behold and bless this Sword of mine, _____."

[Candidate does so.]

May every holy angel come from every quarter and assist this true Companion as he/she asks for aid in any difficulty or in danger when they call upon the name of _____. Be this so, according to the Law which we have here agreed to honor and defend. SO MAY THIS BE, AMEN.

Preceptor: [to Candidate] Now stand in the center as we

indicate, and there receive the contact of our Cross of Steel.

[Candidate stands in the center of the Pentagram, while the Preceptor and the Pontifex stand immediately back and front with the Pontifex before. They both hold their drawn Swords at the carry in their right hands.]

Pontifex: **In the name of Elohim Gibor, Archangel Khamael, the Angel Order of the Seraphim, the Sphere of Mars, and under the authority of Michael, Prince Commander of the Heavenly Hosts, receive this recognition as a bearer of the Sword within the Holy Mysteries of Light and all allied thereto. May your Sword be unto you as those of ancient fame have been to their heroic and immortal users. May the powers proceeding from these Great Ones of the Sword and all your predecessors on this Path pass through this point of contact and be with you now and evermore. Be thou summoned, O ye Strong Ones, by this five-fold clashing of our Swords above the head of our Companion who here forms the focus of our true and trusty Cross of Steel.**

[Preceptor and Pontifex clash their Swords together above the Candidate's head.]

All: [chanting] **One for the Oldest.**

[Clash.]

Two for the Wisest.

[Clash.]

Three for the Surest.

[Clash.]

Four for the Kindest.

[Clash.]

Five for the Bravest.

[Clash and hold a moment.]

HOLD THOU FAST. Well and truly hast thou done, O faithful one. Thanks be. You may stand easy.

Preceptor: **Friend and Companion, sheathe your Sword in Peace; here is its scabbard.**

[Presents it.]

Wear it worthily. By this sign is the Sword invoked amongst us.

[Gives sign.]

Always with the words: "In the Name of the All-Highest, I await my orders." The knocks are five, given metal against metal in this way.

[Sounds them.]

For the present time, you must be diligent and also now obedient to these orders. Do as you are shown. Attention. Handle Sword. Draw Sword. Carry Sword. Rest Sword. Here is your first tour of duty in the service of these Holy Mysteries. It is to guard them well against all profanation and to hold their honor as your own. Give salutes or raise alarms as the occasion may demand. Deal with what you can, or summon aid where necessary. Never try to cope beyond your capabilities. Remember this before all else: Use not the weapon in your hand, but that which it suggests within your consciousness. Think upon and understand this well, for it is a major key within this mystery. Here then is the perimeter and pentacle which you must pace upon patrol. Follow out the paths as they are marked. Deosil invokes; widdershins banishes.

Commencing in the East with carried Sword, pace out the pentagon and then the pentacle. That is the pattern for all operations of the Sword. When you have completed this, again take station at the eastern point and then repeat the exercise as may be necessary until you are relieved of duty or called into action. Now, by the left, forward march!

[During this patrol, the Mars Suite from Holst's *The Planets* is played, or some other appropriate music. There is a noisy Alarm sounded on termination.]

Preceptor: The enemy is at our gates! The enemy is at our gates! The enemy is at our gates! To arms! To arms! Sentinel, our ancient enemy approaches. More harm has reached us from that single source than from any other. Fear this enemy above all else and learn to deal with it accordingly. Know the enemy for what it is and how it threatens. Learn how to conquer and control its conduct. Face it bravely and defend us truly from it. Have you the courage to confront its terror and engage with it in actual combat? Are you brave enough to learn its fearful name? Strong men have died in this encounter, thousands are enslaved for lifetimes, and millions more have no defense at all against an enemy so strong and subtle. Will you really learn the truth at last and meet it face to face? Speak quickly—yes or no—but do not hesitate or falter.

Candidate: Yes.

Preceptor: Then open for yourself the covers of that casement; there you will see and recognize the worst of all that you will meet within our Mysteries. May Heaven help you bear the blow.

[Candidate obeys and faces a mirror inside a curtained casement effect. This is normally on the north wall or convenient blank spot—perhaps behind a door. Eventually . . .]

Preceptor: **Have you seen and have you understood?**

Candidate: **I have.**

Preceptor: **Then help us to combat the common enemy of all who are united in our Mysteries. It is the Dark and dreadful Dweller on the Threshold who prevents our progress on our paths. This is the evil in ourselves, personified as an existence which remains unknown while it conceals itself behind the focus of our consciousness. We cannot face it save by reflection in a magic mirror. Recollect the fable of the Gorgon's head and meditate upon that mystery well. Stand thou here beside us in the common ranks of your companions, and together we shall conquer and defeat the Dweller sheltering within each one of us. Companion, let us be armed and then advance against it.**

Preceptor and Pontifex alternately: **We will assume the armor of the strong in Spirit. Blessed be the special properties of its protection.**

May it save us from assault and prove a sure defense against all evil entities who seek our downfall and destruction.

Let our hearts be guarded by the breastplates of devotion and our heads be within the helmets of discrimination.

On our hands the gauntlets of decisive action and to our feet the shoes of dedicated discipline.

Let our legs be covered with the greaves of steadfastness;
and our shoulders bear the pauldrons of responsibility.

May every link of mail be joined together by the work of
love; so shall we all survive against the forces of annihila-
tion.

Beneath the Shield of our Eternal Guardian we seek safe
shelter.

Blessed be the aegis interposed between ourselves and
our undoing, Holy and Omnipotent the Power proclaimed upon its blazon.

Certain is the Victory to whosoever fights with faith in its
protection.

Blessed be the shining blade we bring to battle.

Liberating is its light, and Beautiful its balance.

Invincible the might behind our Sword of Spirit, and un-
defeatable the Power projected from its point of purpose.

Even as iniquity is rent asunder by its edge, be corruption
cut away from foul encroachment on our healthiness.

Let the challenge of commencement now be sounded
with a note of confidence, that with the aid of every angel
we may fight and conquer.

[Challenge sounded. All assume battle stations.]

THE BATTLE

All: Stand thou forth from us, O Ancient Enemy of Man,
hitherto disguised by darkness. No longer are we unaware of thine existence. Thou deceitful one who

dwelleth on the very threshold of our Portals. Detain us not, but be thou banished in the mighty name of Michael. O thou that art the worst of everything within us. Be conquered by the Circle Cross of our Creation and the spiritual Sign of Cosmos. Be broken by the five-rayed Star of Light we bear upon our breasts in battle, and retreat before our Lances penetrate the persiflage of thy pretenses. We seek to slay thee, not with wanton wastefulness, but to subdue thee in the service of the Holy Ones who work with wisdom. Straight through thee we will follow up our final stroke. Behind thee lies the welcome way of our attainment. With our Shield of Faith, we intercept thy hardest blows. We shall avoid the poisoned arrows of thine animosity. Undaunted by thy wicked weapons, we advance unflinchingly.

Guide, O Great Ones, these our hands in this our conflict. We parry now the dart of thy deadly spear, O Evil Enemy. Be thou circumvented by the Laws of Light within the circle of thy limitations. We strike thee with the sideways stroke of sheer determination. Severed be thy hateful hold upon our human hearts and inmost inclinations. We cleave thee with a cut between the heavens and the Earth. Be thou divided duly, even unto thy destruction. Broken be thy bondage of our intellect and intuition.

Set our spirits free forever from the fetters of thy forging. Prevent no more our progress on our Paths. We have pierced thy center with the thrust of total Truth. Henceforth, be obedient to the Voice of Verity. Accept and answer the authority of the Almighty. Be the Word of Victory announced and held in honor.

EE OH HE WA. IPI HU RA HE. IPI HU RA HE. IPI HU RA HE.

Preceptor: **Companion, sheathe your Sword in honor. It is Peace at last.**

[This is done.]

Welcome, true soldier and defender of these Holy Mysteries. Long live our true and Faithful King, Commander of our Order of Creation.

All: **FOREVER AND FOREVERMORE, AMEN.**

Preceptor: **Now let us celebrate the closing of our Temple as our custom so ordains.**

All: **So will we all. Amen.**

CHAPTER 6

APPLIED PSYCHIC SELF-DEFENSE IN EVERYDAY SITUATIONS

THUS FAR YOU HAVE been 1) Educated as to why psychic self-defense could be important to you (chapter 1); 2) Introduced to basic exercises which, if practiced faithfully, will make it much more difficult for someone to affect your visible and/or invisible bodies without your knowledge and consent (chapter 2); 3) Instructed on the difference between psychic self-defense and spiritual survival, as well as the need to develop a personal relationship with Divinity, by whatever Name(s) you know It, if you are determined to pursue the art of psychic self-defense past the basics (chapter 3); 4) Shown how to recognize the symptoms of psychic disturbance and/or attack and how to bring relief to the victims thereof (chapter 4); 5) Given knowledge of and access to the realms of the Spiritual Warrior (chapter 5).

Before reading any further, please review any of the previous chapters that you may have skimmed or simply not taken the time to digest completely. The rest of this chapter is dedicated to testing your skills under relatively safe real-world conditions. Therefore, it is imperative that you gain at least some proficiency in these skills before going any further.

You will not need to look far to find people who are in the habit of trying to manipulate others to their own advantage. The average salesperson is trained to do exactly that. So what has your sales resistance got to do with the art of psychic self-defense? Everything!

Go ahead; pick out something you have no intention of buying, either because you don't need it or honestly can't afford it, whether you need it or not. The bigger the ticket price, the better. Now, put yourself in the way of a well-trained salesperson whose livelihood depends on selling this very same item. Leave your checkbook, money, and credit cards at home. Take a friend along if you think you may need either a witness or back-up. After allowing the salesperson to work his craft on you while using whatever you have going for you at this point to resist his abilities, excuse yourself and answer the following questionnaire honestly.

1. How long did it take the salesperson to establish a rapport with you? (When did you find yourself beginning to relax in his presence and/or agreeing with some of his statements concerning the benefits of his product in general or to you personally?)

2. Did you at any time find yourself nodding "yes" to a product you already knew you didn't need, want, or couldn't afford?

3. At any time, did you find yourself sitting or standing, facing the salesperson with the centerline of your body completely open to him or her?

4. Did you feel the need to cover up any of your psychic centers during the sales presentation?

5. Did you actually do so?

6. When you left the sales office/floor did you take the salesperson's business card (just to be polite or unconsciously)? Did you promise to "think about it" or get back to the salesperson later?

7. If you had access to your money, checkbook, or credit cards, would you have tried to find some way that you could afford whatever the product was, even if you didn't need or want it, and especially if you knew you really couldn't afford it?

Unless you have already taken the time (at least 6 months) to develop a set of extremely strong psychic shields through the practice of the exercises that were presented in the previous chapters, or by the longterm practice of similar exercises that you learned somewhere else, you will find your answers to the above questionnaire rather disappointing. Well, now that you have most likely fallen off this horse, get right back on it and try again. This time, however, begin by emptying your pockets of all tobacco products and/or any items that may tend to weaken you. (If the salesperson asks you if you mind if he or she smokes, tell him, yes, you do mind.) Wear or carry a garnet. Make sure you have eaten a healthy meal within the last hour and a half. Next, remind yourself at regular intervals that the decision to buy or not is yours and that you have already determined not to do so. Stand or sit during the sales presentation with your feet touching, your hands interlocked (loosely) and resting on your solar plexus. Allow your elbows to touch your ribs and mentally center and ground yourself. You should find that you do much better this time. In fact, the salesperson (if well trained) will not spend much time with you at all as long as you stick to the program outlined above.

Please note: I am not attempting to put you off salespeople or presentations. I am simply using them as a valuable real-world resource. My daughter has sold women's dresses at Sears; I have owned several businesses which required a good deal of salesmanship; and one of my dearest friends is a very successful used-car salesman. Most people who earn their living through sales are goodhearted and really don't want to rip anyone off. Unfortunately, when personal survival or greed is at stake, many salespeople will cross the line between simply doing their job and out-and-out psychic coercion. "Let the buyer beware!" takes on a whole new meaning under these conditions.

Once you have managed to get in and out of a sales presentation of the kind described above in under five minutes, you can pat yourself on the back. Now the trick is to do just as well when you are confronted with a similar situation that you have not deliberately set up and for which you are not prepared. Just like anything else that you learn, it will take time to make this behavior into a habit that your subconscious mind can handle for you completely. The only way to make this happen is to practice, practice, and keep practicing!

Salesmanship is not the only thing against which you must develop psychic shields in your daily life if you want to insure that you are not being psychically manipulated into doing something against your "better/conscious judgment." Pick up any book by John Grinder and Richard Bandler on the subjects of neuro-linguistic programming (NLP) or hypnosis and you will see how easy it is for other people to alter your state of awareness just enough to slip past your conscious mind. Now those techniques have some very valuable therapeutic applications, but, in the wrong hands, they can be easily misused.

I have taken intensive courses in hypnosis which were very well attended. It was very informative to find that most of the other students were members of one of the human-service professions (social workers, psychologists, therapists, nurses, priests, ministers, etc.). With very little practice, even the most socially inept of the group was able to alter the state of consciousness of someone to whom they were merely speaking in the most casual of circumstances. I had the opportunity to talk to a number of these people several months later and found that, like myself, they had continued to practice the techniques they had learned and had been putting them to mostly good use. One lady did go a bit overboard in her use of these techniques on her family. It seems she was tired of dealing with a difficult teenage daughter on the issue of doing daily chores. This hard-working mother found it far easier to reframe her daughter's behavior a bit more to her liking, regardless of the ethics involved. As the mother of two teenage daughters, I'm not sure I blame her!

OK, on to your next exercise! This one is only for those of you with liberal political and economic leanings. Pick up a copy of Ayn Rand's *Atlas Shrugged*. If you have never read it before, so much the better. Read this novel the way you would read any other fiction book. Notice if you find yourself agreeing with an economic, or any other, philosophy that is not normally your own. This can happen easily when a writer is good at establishing a strong rapport between the reader and the main characters in a novel. Since most people read novels with all of their defenses down (after all, they are perfectly safe in their own homes aren't they?), it is very easy for authors to gain access to more of you through their books than you would allow if you saw them in person (unless of course, you are a celebrity junkie). Next, pick up any other novel by the same author and prepare yourself to read it critically and objectively. Remind yourself why you believe whatever your personal and economic philosophies are, and why they are appropriate to you. Make sure you read in a seated position rather than lying down. Drink your favorite stimulating beverage (coffee, tea, hot chocolate, or soda) while you read. You may even set an alarm clock so that you read for no more than an hour at a time. You will probably find that this exercise is less satisfying as a reading experience, but you will also find that you are much more consciously aware of the author's political and economic agendas.

Those of you with a more conservative political and economic outlook may do exactly what I suggested above, substituting two novels by another author, as long as that author normally expresses philosophies opposite to your own through the medium of his or her main characters. You might try the Darkover novels by Marian Zimmer Bradley if you can't think of anything else, although these are not really in the same league as Ayn Rand's books.

Television programs, radio and TV advertisements, movies, infomercials, political speeches, polls of any kind presented by a supposedly neutral news anchor, and talk shows of all varieties are all capable of affecting your subconscious mind and thereby your physical activities. How much and to what effect depends largely on how well they are designed to do exactly this and how open you are to their manipulation. Test yourself on some of the less threatening of these media presentations. Practice until you no longer need to make an outward show of control in order to maintain your shields.

Actually, just about any activity that involves your interaction with someone else has the potential for mutual manipulation. We all affect each other simply by the very act of sharing a conversation or being in close proximity. There is really no need to become paranoid about what others can do to you. You have the sensitivity-training exercises which were presented earlier in this book which you can practice until you are capable of recognizing the slightest tug on your aura. Once you notice the tug, you can either disengage the other party's link with you or, better yet, investigate what it is they appear to want from you.

Some people need the attention of others just to feel reasonably good about themselves. Some people require more than mere attention. Some may need healing on one or more levels and simply not know how to go about getting it. You need to know whether you wish to spend time giving these people what they need or not.

If you are like most of us, you have the natural desire to help and heal when you can. Also, like most people, you may not know how to do this without virtually giving away pieces of yourself. The following is an exercise in energy projection that makes use of what might best be called universal or cosmic energy which is available to all beings. Learning to project this universal energy rather than your personal vital life force is essential if you wish to help and heal without weakening yourself. Psychic healers and psychic advisers would do well to pay attention to this exercise. In my experience with these well-meaning people, they often end up tired and debilitated after working. If they knew how to project only *universal* energy, working would actually leave them more energetic than they were before they started.

EXERCISE 11
The Unbendable Arm

1. Choose a partner who is obviously bigger and stronger than yourself.

2. Stand with your right shoulder facing the centerline of your partner's body (you are standing at a 90-degree angle to each other). Place the outside edge of your right wrist on your partner's left shoulder and adjust your relative distance until your right arm is out straight, but relaxed. Keep your right hand open.

3. Bend your knees slightly and take the time to Center and Ground yourself.

4. Ask your partner to place his or her hands gently over the place where your right arm would normally bend. Since your elbow will be pointing toward the floor, your partner's hands will rest on top of the inside of your elbow (see figure 6, page 78).

5. Visualize and feel yourself drawing universal energy from the Earth below you, up through your feet, up

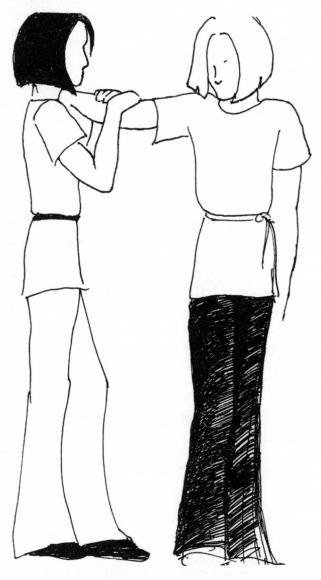

Figure 6. The Unbendable Arm Exercise.

through your body, until it reaches your Fire Center, from which you will channel it out through your right arm and the fingers of your right hand. Next visualize and feel yourself drawing universal energy down from the heavens above you, down through the crown of your head, down into your body until it reaches your Fire Center, from which you will channel it out through your right arm and the fingers of your right hand. The feeling will be something like turning on a hydrant to feed a firehose (your right arm). As long as this "hydrant" is turned on, universal energy will come into your body and shoot out the fingers of your right hand in such a way as to make your arm as unbendable as a firehose would be if the hydrant feeding it were turned on full blast.

6. Ask your partner to attempt to bend your right arm while applying steady downward pressure (no jerking of your arm is allowed, as that can injure your joint) with as much force as possible. You will need to keep the visualizations and feelings described in Step 5 going while your partner does this. The result should be that your arm is virtually unbendable, even though it is physically relaxed. You should actually be able to pat your partner's neck or pull his or her hair (gently) while the attempt is made to bend your arm.

7. Now try this exercise again, but start and end with the relative strength test you were taught in Exercise 1 (page 3). After practicing the Unbendable Arm Exercise you should be as strong as or stronger than you were before you attempted it.

I have even taught 6-year old children to do this exercise successfully. So go ahead and give it a go! Actually, the fact that your arm can't be bent easily by even a much stronger person is not really the point of this exercise. That result simply confirms that you are projecting something through your arm in such a way as to keep it from bending. That something is the universal/cosmic energy that is available to all living things. By taking it in through your body in quantities beyond your personal requirements and then projecting it out through your right hand, you have learned the basic technique you will need to send energy to others who need it. With practice, you should be able to "color" this energy to help and heal in rather specific ways.

If you are thinking that this technique could be misused, you are right. However, people attempting to do so need to "color" the universal energy for unpleasant purposes while that energy is still inside them. This could lead to a very unfortunate case of psychic indigestion or self-poisoning, especially if the target simply refuses the energy. If you have ever witnessed what happens when a sewer drain backs up into a bathroom, you will have a good idea what this can be like. Needless to say, most "baddies" don't tempt this fate often.

Table 2 gives a list of positive colors and their associations which can be used to "tint" the universal energy that you wish to send to someone in need.

Table 2. Positive Colors and their Associations.

COLOR	PURPOSE
Indigo	Stability
Purple	Prosperity, Spiritual growth
Bright Red	Will power, Vitality
Orange	Success, Power, Illumination
Emerald Green	Love, Pleasure, Beauty
Yellow	Good Business, Communication
Blue	Dealing with the public and healing

CHAPTER 7

APPLIED PSYCHIC SELF-DEFENSE IN NON-ORDINARY SITUATIONS, INCLUDING "THE BATTLE ARCANE"

THE LAST CHAPTER included what were, for the most part, the "fail-safe" ways of testing your ability to defend yourself psychically. This chapter is written with the experienced magical and/or spiritual practitioner in mind. If you do not have the training or experience required, do not even *think* about using the methods described in this chapter. If you wish to gain the appropriate magical training, excellent manuals have been written by Wm. G. Gray, Israel Regardie, Donald Tyson, Denning and Phillips, and Alan Richardson, to name just a few. Excellent spiritual training can be acquired through reputable seminaries and the like, or, failing that, there are plenty of good books written by spiritual leaders of the world's numerous religious systems.

Whether you plan to read this chapter purely for information or for the purpose of adding to your personal experience, first go back and reread chapter 5. Pay special attention to the ritual named "Gaining the Sword." Absorb the symbolism and reality which is the Sword of the Spiritual Warrior. Note that you will have to conquer the darkness in yourself before you are likely to conquer it in others. Since this could take a lifetime or more, you must learn to use your Sword to neutralize the malefic intentions others may have toward you or anyone you are protecting.

For most of you, the likelihood of actually fighting a spiritual/psychic/magical duel or even needing to neutralize the effects of nasty thought-forms or spells directed at you and those you protect is almost nil. However, simply because a situation is unlikely to occur, we are not excused from being prepared for it if we are capable and feel called to do so.

Please refer back to the Middle Pillar Exercise (Exercise 10, page 20). This exercise can be expanded to make it a very effective and practical magical magnet for your specific needs. It also is an important component in serious spiritual/psychic/magical self-defense.

EXERCISE 12

Expanded Middle Pillar Exercise

1. Begin by taking a shower with the intention of purifying yourself spiritually as well as physically. (Check out the Draining Exercise on page 18).

2. Dress in clean, loose clothing. Stand with your hands resting on the hilt of your Sword. (It should be unsheathed and positioned so that its tip touches the floor slightly in front of and directly between your two feet.) Now work the Middle Pillar Exercise as it was described in chapter 2.

3. Once the energy is circulating throughout your psychic body, visualize your energy colored an appropriate shade to become a magnet for whatever you need (see Table 2 on page 80).

4. If what you need requires bringing something into your life, visualize the universal energies connected with your need as being drawn into your psychic body. You will attract this with the "negative" color associated with your

need. (Note: The words "positive" and "negative" refer to polarized charges such as those found in protons and electrons. They do *not* equate with "good" and "evil.") If what you need involves sending something to someone else, visualize the energies which originate in you coloring the universal energy that you draw into yourself with the "positive" color associated with your need. This energy must then be projected out toward your target using a method similar to the one described in The Unbendable Arm Exercise (see page 77). The only difference will be that you use your Sword as an extension of your right arm to send this energy on its way.

Should you need to combat abusive and/or evil intentions directed at you by means of sorcery or the like, create a safe place in which you can evaluate the situation objectively. You learned the method of purifying and sealing a place in chapter 4. Again, it may be necessary to expand upon this by actually setting up a magic circle, unless you have access to a permanently consecrated space (a personal Temple for example). This may be accomplished by working the Lesser Banishing Ritual of the Pentagram as described in chapter 5 (see page 46) or some other ritual which will fulfill the same purpose. At the appropriate place in this ritual, ask for clear sight and guidance concerning the presumed threat. You may use whatever divinatory aids you need including such things as tarot cards. You need to find out whether you or whoever you have agreed to help really are under attack. Once this has been confirmed, you need to have some idea of what will neutralize the attack. (Knowing exactly what has been sent your way is important. You may need to use divination to find this out.) When this has been accomplished, you may use the expanded form of the Middle Pillar Exercise which was described earlier in this chapter to complete the work (see page 82). When this is done, you can finish the Pentagram Ritual with absolute faith in your success.

Table 3. Positive and Negative Color Chart.

POSITIVE	NEGATIVE	PURPOSE
Indigo	Black	Stability Rectifying Abuses
Purple	Blue	Prosperity Generosity Spirituality Expansion
Bright Red	Bright Red	Construction Destruction Protection Vitality Magnetism Will Power
Orange	Yellow or Gold	Power Success Balance Beauty Illumination
Emerald Green	Emerald Green	Love Social Affairs Pleasure The Arts
Yellow	Orange	Business Success Communication Intelligence
Blue	Puce	Fertility General Public Change Healing

Sounds pretty simple, doesn't it? Well it is, if you have courage and unfailing faith! Unfortunately, most people are prone to fear. Especially if you are trying to help people out of sticky situations, fear (theirs or yours) may be a very real threat to the success of your work.

Because fear and lack of faith can cause so much trouble, it will be very necessary for you to understand the cultural and religious background of those with whom you deal, whether they are attackers or victims. I know of people who have quite literally refused to get better after receiving a medical treatment that Western science had proven to be effective for their condition. This was a case of mind over matter. These patients had been brought up to believe that only something they considered "hot" could cure their particular illness and they were being treated with something that they considered "cold"! Since they didn't believe the treatment could work, it didn't! Imagine how much more important cultural and/or religious beliefs can be in relation to our subject.

The paragraph above should make it clear why it is rather important to understand the use of such things as amulets, talismans, oils, candles, incense, potions, and the like, if you choose to be a "knight in shining armor" for other humans. There is nothing wrong with—and everything to be gained—using folk remedies for psychic attacks and/or disturbances, so long as you also use your common sense and the other methods described in this book. Works by authors such as Anna Riva, Scott Cunningham, Migene Gonzalez-Whippler, and Israel Regardie can all be helpful should you need to upgrade your understanding of this type of approach.

For the most part, when you must deal with attacks and attackers, it is only really necessary to disconnect yourself from their playing field and to ignore them. This is harder than it sounds, but doing "nothing" is often the very best thing you can do. Of course, you must have mastered any fears you may have in relation to these "attacks" and have absolute faith in the effectiveness of cutting the ties that bind you to the attacker.

The ties that bind you to anything or anyone may be forged by yourself, the other participant, or even both parties simultaneously. They may have been established during this lifetime or during one long since past. The Sword is just the thing to use to cut these ties cleanly. Once this is done, it is up to you to move on with your life and never look back. Any attention paid to the source of the attack after the ties between attacker and victim have been severed will only serve to allow those ties to be regenerated.

The process of cutting the ties between attacker and victim may be used either within or outside a magic circle. If you plan to use a magic circle, you must choose something to symbolize your attacker. Tie a red string or piece of yarn (several feet long) to it. The symbol (perhaps just a piece of paper with the attacker's name on it or even the words "attacker of _____") will be left outside the area the magic circle will occupy, preferably inside a triangle. The string represents the connection between victim and attacker. It will be stretched to touch the perimeter of your magic circle (it must not enter the circle). Make sure the symbol and attached string are on nonflammable surfaces (placing them on top of a heavy layer of aluminum foil will do in most cases). Now follow these directions:

1. Take a purification shower and dress in clean clothes.

2. Purify and seal the area in which you will establish your magic circle.

3. Perform The Lesser Banishing Ritual of the Pentagram of Earth using your Sword. In the appropriate place, ask for strength, guidance, and protection as you cut the ties that bind you to your attacker. Work the expanded form of the Middle Pillar Exercise to establish these qualities in yourself and then end the Pentagram Ritual.

4. Walk up to the edge of the circle that the red string touches. Slice across its end with your Sword, intending to sever all ties. Finally, set fire to the string and watch as it burns back to its source.

5. Throw a piece of black silk over whatever is left of the symbol and use that silk to pick it up and dispose of it, burying it in the earth or throwing it into a clean body of running water.

6. After disposing of the above, you must not talk to anyone about what you did or about the attacker and his effects on you prior to this ritual. Simply walk away and never look back, having absolute faith that you have accomplished your goal.

If you choose to use a more direct method of severing the ties between yourself or another and a "baddie," it would still be wise to take a purification bath, dress in clean clothes, and use the expanded form of the Middle Pillar Exercise to bring into you any of the qualities you will need to successfully perform your task. After this has been done, visualize the ties that bind you or whomever you are protecting to the attacker. Use your Sword to cut these cleanly, and then mentally cauterize each end. The end closest to whoever is the target of the attack will blacken, dry up, and fall off in very short order. If the end still attached to the attacker does not do likewise, you may mentally set fire to it, intending it to burn away only the tie. Once this has been accomplished, all parties are free and the former target must avoid reestablishing contact with the attacker by thoughts, words, or deeds from then on.

Occasionally, it is more expedient to absorb an unpleasant thoughtform and convert its energy from that which has been harassing you to something which will help you and thereby weaken the sender. This is a much more advanced form of what you practiced in the very first exercise in this book. If you can temporarily weaken your adversary in this way, he will often need a good deal of time to restore his constitution on all levels. During this time, he will doubtless think twice about creating further problems for you or in your sphere of influence. It's simply too much work for too little pay-off! He may even warn other unpleasant types off "your turf" for the same reason.

The major drawback to this approach is that you may not be strong enough to separate adversary from energy, even at long range, in which case you will experience some rather severe psychic/magical indigestion and may become quite ill. The age-old charge to all spiritual practitioners to "know yourself" is very important when working with this level of force and form.

THE GUARDIANS

There is an order of spiritual practitioners known as the Guardians, who seek to serve both Divinity and Humanity. Their symbol is the Sword. The Guardians are a Warrior-Priest order dedicated to preserve, protect, and promote the Way of Light within this world. They are duty-bound to do Good and avert Evil. Guardians may be of any religious faith, so long as that faith is consistent with the goals stated above.

The Guardians recognize four basic levels of membership or rank. These levels are based on ability, training, and personal dedication to the Cause. The four levels are as follows:

WATCHERS: This is the entry level rank. Watchers are charged to:

    1. Watch what other members do.

2. Learn through training sessions the basics of physical and spiritual self-defense.

3. Warn senior members if and when they notice or come across a situation that requires specialized attention.

Note: Watchers train for at least a year and a day before being considered for any other duties. During this time, they will get to know more about The Guardians and will be better able to determine if this Path is one that they can walk in good faith.

WARDERS: Warders are those members who have successfully completed the basic training given to the Watchers and have subsequently agreed to take on the increased responsibility of this rank. Warders are charged to perfect their skills through continued training. They will be expected to help train the Watchers by making themselves available when necessary to demonstrate techniques, answer questions, and offer encouragement and advice in a brotherly or sisterly fashion. They are also expected to see to the basic protection of themselves and their loved ones. Warders are taught to be aware of what they do know and, more importantly, of what they don't know. They must learn to defer to higher authority when necessary. Finally, Warders are expected to explore and practice the three qualities of the true Warrior—honor, courage, and duty.

GUARDIANS: The rank of Guardian is the first level of true knighthood. Guardians earn their consecrated Sword at this level of membership and take on the responsibilities of senior officers and instructors within the Order. If the member has not to this point been ordained in some form of priesthood, this will occur at this point, unless there is some outstanding and exceptional reason why this should not be done. Guardians are charged to teach both Watchers and Warders the required curricula of those grades and review all serious requests for active intervention against Evil as it plays out in this world. Before sanctioning any action, Guardians must ordinarily refer the matter to the Council of Masters with their recommendations. A firm stance against purely personal quarrels must be maintained. In dire necessity and the absence of a Master or the Council of Masters, Guardians may take on the responsibility to act should this become absolutely necessary. Elevation to the rank of Guardian is based solely on the recommendation of the Council of Masters.

MASTERS: Masters of the Order are those members who have proved themselves over time and through effort to exemplify the ideals of the Order. Their job is to administer, teach, train, and take the final responsibility for the work of The Guardians within this world. On their shoulders rests the burden of deciding when combat is necessary and justified. Elevation to the rank of Master requires unanimous acclamation of the Council of Masters.

REQUIREMENTS FOR BECOMING A GUARDIAN

1. You must be old enough to understand the meaning of your commitment, but not so old that you have lost the flexibility to change significantly for the better. Normally this means you must be at least 25 years old and under 70 years of age. However, each applicant is judged on a case by case basis.

2. You must believe in some Source of All Existence. While most people call this Being "God," you must be flexible enough to understand that any version of this Being (however named and understood by other individuals and re-

gardless of whether It be acknowledged as One or Many Beings) which provides a stable spiritual foundation for a given individual is as valid as any other that does the same.

3. You must be in good physical and mental health. This means that any condition that is likely to prove de-stabilizing and/or cause psychological problems would disqualify an applicant from membership. The job of The Guardians in this world requires a good deal of physical, mental, emotional, and spiritual stability and balance. Although this may be worked on and developed over time, any condition that seriously inhibits its growth in applicants puts them at considerable risk.

4. You must be able to commit 2 to 5 hours a day to your training and development without neglecting your responsibilities to family and friends. This will include training in physical and psychic self-defense, meditation, prayer, academic pursuits, and good works.

5. You must have a quiet, clean, place to which you can retire for personal training, prayer, meditation, etc. which is free of distractions from the mundane world. Part of this should function as a Temple, part as a study, and part as a physical workout space.

6. You must agree to be upright in your personal habits. This includes sexual ethics: No casual or meaningless mating for the sheer relief of bodily functions is worthy of the state or goals of a Guardian. (Sexual relations with someone you love and trust and with whom you wish to share the joy of living are of course to be encouraged, according to the wills of the parties involved.)

7. You must be willing to "Know Yourself." This means examining your conscience and recognizing your faults and

failings as well as your better personal propensities on a regular basis.

8. You must be willing to command the worst side of yourself to serve the best side of yourself.

My greatest wish for those of you who have read this book and used it as it was intended, as a training manual, is that you will never *need* to use the knowledge and techniques you have acquired therefrom. However, if you want to learn more of the arts of the Spiritual Warrior, you may contact me through the publisher of this book. If you wish to apply for training with the Guardians, please read the above list of requirements for membership again and take the time to meditate on how they will change your life. If you still feel called to apply for membership and training, you may contact me about this also through the publisher of this book.

May the God(s) of your heart bless and keep you safe.

APPENDIX A

DAILY PSYCHIC AWARENESS
AND SELF-DEFENSE EXERCISE FORMS

These forms are meant to be used with Exercises 1 through 12.

Name:_____Date:_____

Time:_____Exercise:_____

Health (circle one)   Excellent, Good, Fair, Poor

Explanatory comments on health:_____

_____

Weather Conditions:_____

Comments on Success of Exercise:_____

_____

Name:_____Date:_____

Time:_____Exercise:_____

Health (circle one)   Excellent, Good, Fair, Poor

Explanatory comments on health:_____

_____

Weather Conditions:_____

Comments on Success of Exercise:_____

_____

- -

Name:_____Date:_____

Time:_____Exercise:_____

Health (circle one)   Excellent, Good, Fair, Poor

Explanatory comments on health:_____

_____

Weather Conditions:_____

Comments on Success of Exercise:_____

_____

Name:_____Date:_____

Time:_____Exercise:_____

Health (circle one)   Excellent, Good, Fair, Poor

Explanatory comments on health:_____

_____

Weather Conditions:_____

Comments on Success of Exercise:_____

_____

Name:_____Date:_____

Time:_____Exercise:_____

Health (circle one)   Excellent, Good, Fair, Poor

Explanatory comments on health:_____

_____

Weather Conditions:_____

Comments on Success of Exercise:_____

_____

Name:_____Date:_____

Time:_____Exercise:_____

Health (circle one)   Excellent, Good, Fair, Poor

Explanatory comments on health:_____

_____

Weather Conditions:_____

Comments on Success of Exercise:_____

_____

- -

Name:_____Date:_____

Time:_____Exercise:_____

Health (circle one)   Excellent, Good, Fair, Poor

Explanatory comments on health:_____

_____

Weather Conditions:_____

Comments on Success of Exercise:_____

_____

Name:_____Date:_____

Time:_____Exercise:_____

Health (circle one)   Excellent, Good, Fair, Poor

Explanatory comments on health:_____

_____

Weather Conditions:_____

Comments on Success of Exercise:_____

_____

Name:_____Date:_____

Time:_____Exercise:_____

Health (circle one)   Excellent, Good, Fair, Poor

Explanatory comments on health:_____

_____

Weather Conditions:_____

Comments on Success of Exercise:_____

_____

Name:_____Date:_____

Time:_____Exercise:_____

Health (circle one)   Excellent, Good, Fair, Poor

Explanatory comments on health:_____

_____

Weather Conditions:_____

Comments on Success of Exercise:_____

_____

- -

Name:_____Date:_____

Time:_____Exercise:_____

Health (circle one)   Excellent, Good, Fair, Poor

Explanatory comments on health:_____

_____

Weather Conditions:_____

Comments on Success of Exercise:_____

_____

Name:_____Date:_____

Time:_____Exercise:_____

Health (circle one)   Excellent, Good, Fair, Poor

Explanatory comments on health:_____

_____

Weather Conditions:_____

Comments on Success of Exercise:_____

_____

Name:_____Date:_____

Time:_____Exercise:_____

Health (circle one)   Excellent, Good, Fair, Poor

Explanatory comments on health:_____

_____

Weather Conditions:_____

Comments on Success of Exercise:_____

_____

Name:_____Date:_____

Time:_____Exercise:_____

Health (circle one)   Excellent, Good, Fair, Poor

Explanatory comments on health:_____

_____

Weather Conditions:_____

Comments on Success of Exercise:_____

_____

- -

Name:_____Date:_____

Time:_____Exercise:_____

Health (circle one)   Excellent, Good, Fair, Poor

Explanatory comments on health:_____

_____

Weather Conditions:_____

Comments on Success of Exercise:_____

_____

APPENDIX B

DAILY JOURNAL OF
SPIRITUAL INSIGHTS FORMS

These forms are to be used as daily journal-keeping guide-lines.

Name:_____Date:_____Time:_____

Hour was dedicated to:_____

Weather Conditions:_____

Personal emotional/mental/physical state:

_____

Description of event/observation/feeling:

_____

_____

Name:_____Date:_____Time:_____

Hour was dedicated to:_____

Weather Conditions:_____

Personal emotional/mental/physical state:

_____

Description of event/observation/feeling:

_____

_____

- -

Name:_____Date:_____Time:_____

Hour was dedicated to:_____

Weather Conditions:_____

Personal emotional/mental/physical state:

_____

Description of event/observation/feeling:

_____

_____

Name:_____Date:_____Time:_____

Hour was dedicated to:_____

Weather Conditions:_____

Personal emotional/mental/physical state:

_____

Description of event/observation/feeling:

_____

_____

Name:_____Date:_____Time:_____

Hour was dedicated to:_____

Weather Conditions:_____

Personal emotional/mental/physical state:

_____

Description of event/observation/feeling:

_____

_____

Name:_____Date:_____Time:_____

Hour was dedicated to:_____

Weather Conditions:_____

Personal emotional/mental/physical state:

_____

Description of event/observation/feeling:

_____

_____

- -

Name:_____Date:_____Time:_____

Hour was dedicated to:_____

Weather Conditions:_____

Personal emotional/mental/physical state:

_____

Description of event/observation/feeling:

_____

_____

Name:_____Date:_____Time:_____

Hour was dedicated to:_____

Weather Conditions:_____

Personal emotional/mental/physical state:

_____

Description of event/observation/feeling:

_____

_____

- -

Name:_____Date:_____Time:_____

Hour was dedicated to:_____

Weather Conditions:_____

Personal emotional/mental/physical state:

_____

Description of event/observation/feeling:

_____

_____

Name:_____Date:_____Time:_____

Hour was dedicated to:_____

Weather Conditions:_____

Personal emotional/mental/physical state:

_____

Description of event/observation/feeling:

_____

_____

Name:_____Date:_____Time:_____

Hour was dedicated to:_____

Weather Conditions:_____

Personal emotional/mental/physical state:

_____

Description of event/observation/feeling:

_____

_____

Name:_____Date:_____Time:_____

Hour was dedicated to:_____

Weather Conditions:_____

Personal emotional/mental/physical state:

_____

Description of event/observation/feeling:

_____

_____

- -

Name:_____Date:_____Time:_____

Hour was dedicated to:_____

Weather Conditions:_____

Personal emotional/mental/physical state:

_____

Description of event/observation/feeling:

_____

_____

Name:_____Date:_____Time:_____

Hour was dedicated to:_____

Weather Conditions:_____

Personal emotional/mental/physical state:

_____

Description of event/observation/feeling:

_____

_____

- -

Name:_____Date:_____Time:_____

Hour was dedicated to:_____

Weather Conditions:_____

Personal emotional/mental/physical state:

_____

Description of event/observation/feeling:

_____

_____

BIBLIOGRAPHY

Anonymous. *The Black Pullet*. New York: Samuel Weiser, 1972.

Barret, Francis. *The Magus*. London: Lackington Allen & Co., 1801.

Blavatsky, H. P. *Isis Unveiled*. Wheaton: Theosophical University Press, 1976.

Bradley, Marian Zimmer. *Leroni of Darkover*. New York: DAW/Penguin, 1991.

———. *To Catch the Trap*. New York: Ballantine, 1984.

Buckland, Raymond. *Buckland's Complete Book of Witchcraft*. St. Paul: Llewellyn, 1986.

Butler, William E. *Apprenticed to Magic*. London: Aquarian Press, 1962.

———. *How to Read the Aura, Practice Psychometry, Telepathy, & Clairvoyance*. Rochester, VT: Destiny/Inner Traditions, 1971.

———. *Magic: Its Ritual, Power and Purpose*. London: Aquarian Press, 1956; New York: Samuel Weiser, 1967.

———. *The Magician: His Training and Work*. N. Hollywood: Wilshire, 1979.

Cavendish, Richard. *The Black Arts*. New York: Perigee/Putnam, 1968.

Cunningham, Scott. *Complete Book of Incense, Oils & Brews*. St. Paul: Llewellyn, 1989.

———. *Cunningham's Encyclopedia of Crystal, Gem & Metal Magic*. St. Paul: Llewellyn, 1987.

———. *Cunningham's Encyclopedia of Magical Herbs*. St. Paul: Llewellyn, 1985.

———. *The Magic in Food: Legends, Lore & Spellwork*. St. Paul: Llewellyn, 1991.

Denning, Melita and Osborne Phillips. *Llewellyn Practical Guide to the Development of Psychic Powers*. St. Paul: Llewellyn, 1981.

———. *Llewellyn Practical Guide to Psychic Self-Defense & Well-Being*. St. Paul: Llewellyn, 1983.

———. *The Magical Philosophy*. 5 vols. St. Paul: Llewellyn, 1974.

Deren, M. *Divine Horseman: The Living Gods of Haiti*. Reprint: Kingston, NY: McPherson & Co., 1984.

Elworthy, Frederick T. *The Evil Eye*. Secaucus, NJ: Citadel, 1982.

Fortune, Dion. *Applied Magic*. London: Aquarian Press, 1962.

———. *Cosmic Doctrine*. London: Aquarian Press, 1976.

———. *Mystical Qabalah*. London: Rider, 1935; Aquarian Press, 1951; York Beach, ME: Samuel Weiser, 1984.

———. *Psychic Self-Defense*. London: Rider, 1930; York Beach, ME: Samuel Weiser, 1992.

Funk, R. W. and R. W. Hoovor, and the Jesus Seminar. *The Five Gospels: The Search for the Authentic Words of Jesus*. New York: Macmillan, 1993.

Gonzalez-Wippler, Migene. *Complete Book of Spells, Ceremonies & Magic*. St. Paul: Llewellyn, 1988.

———. *Santeria: The Religion*. New York: Harmony/Crown, 1989.

Gray, William G. *Between Good and Evil: Polarities of Power*. St. Paul: Llewellyn, 1989.

———. *Ladder of Lights*. Cheltenham, England: Helios, 1968; York Beach, ME: Samuel Weiser, 1981.

———. *Magical Ritual Methods*. Cheltenham, England: Helios, 1971; York Beach, ME: Samuel Weiser, 1980.

———. *Rite of Light*. Albany, NY: Privately printed, 1976.

———. *Tree of Evil*. York Beach, ME: Samuel Weiser, 1984.

Grinder, John and Richard Bandler. *Trance-Formations: Neuro-Linguistic Programming & the Structure of Hypnosis*. Moab, UT: Real People Press, 1993.

Hope, Murry. *Practical Techniques of Psychic Self-Defense*. New York: St. Martins, 1985.

Huson, Paul. *Mastering Witchcraft*. New York: Perigee/Putnam, 1980.

Martin, Malachi. *Hostage to the Devil*. New York: Harper-Collins, 1987.

Rand, Ayn. *Atlas Shrugged*. New York: NAL/Dutton, 1992.

Regardie, Israel. *The Complete Golden Dawn System of Magic*. Phoenix, AZ: New Falcon Press, 1984.

———. *The Golden Dawn*. 4 vols. St. Paul: Llewellyn, 1969, 1986.

———. *How to Make and Use Talismans*. London: Aquarian Press, 1972; New York: Samuel Weiser, 1972.

Riva, Anna. *Golden Secrets of Mystical Oils Revised*. Los Angeles: International Imports, 1990.

———. *Modern Herbal Spellbook*. Los Angeles: International Imports, 1985.

———. *Powers of the Psalms*. Los Angeles: International Imports, 1982.

Tyson, D. *The New Magus: A Modern Magician's Practical Guide*. St. Paul: Llewellyn, 1987.

———. *Ritual Magic: What It Is and How to Do It*. St. Paul: Llewellyn, 1992.

INDEX

Marcia L. Pickands is a remarkably versatile teacher, with training in psychology, theology, ceremonial magic, and many other esoteric, metaphysical, and magical topics. In addition to her twenty-five years experience as a psychic and spiritual adviser, and her eighteen years as a mother, she has worked as an archeological technician, an historic artifact analyst, a New Age bookstore owner, a Neo-Pagan High Priestess, and a martial arts master and teacher. She is one of the two spiritual successors to the late William G. Gray, renowned author of many fine books on magic and the Western Inner Tradition, and serves as the Warden of the Sangreal Sodality. In addition, Ms. Pickands is the current Senior Master of the Guardians, a Warrior-Priest Order dedicated to preserving, protecting, and promoting the Way of Light within this world by doing Good and averting Evil.

"The numerous hats I have worn and continue to wear within this world," she comments, "have given me a rather unique viewpoint. I have experienced firsthand the need to be ready and able to protect both myself and those for whom I have been responsible. While the martial arts certainly provide some very useful techniques for doing exactly that," she adds, "they are not always appropriate. That's how I discovered the value of psychic self-defense."